Independent Buses in North Wales

Neville Mercer

© 2012 Venture Publications Ltd

ISBN 978 1905 304 486

CONTENTS

By the Same author

Independent Buses in Shropshire
Independent Buses in Staffordshire

INTRODUCTION

My maternal grandparents, Joseph and Beatrice Street, were well known to everyone who attended the small primary school in Wincham, a village two miles to the northeast of the market town of Northwich in Cheshire. He was the part-time caretaker (during the day he worked as a labourer at the 'Selva' salt-works) while she served as the solitary dinner-lady and fed most of the school's four dozen pupils at lunchtime.

As a result she knew everybody in the village and the surrounding countryside, and in the late 1940s began to organise a programme of community coach outings. Every trip was dutifully recorded by my grandfather's ancient 'Box Brownie', and at least one photograph in each set would show the assembled passengers posing alongside the coach. From being a babe in arms I was always in the photograph and this may well have sparked my lifelong interest in the bus and coach industry.

Until 1959 (when the firm ceased to trade) the vehicles would be hired from Bowyers of Northwich and the earliest shots in her 'outings' album featured that company's two Foden PVSC6s with Trans-United bodywork. Sadly, these were sold before I was born and my baby pictures showed me being carried onto Bedford OB and SB types with Duple bodies.

By the time that I went to the school myself I had already acquired a basic knowledge of the North Western Road Car Company's fleet by watching their vehicles passing through the village – there wasn't much else to do unless Manchester (Ringway) airport was using Runway 06 which brought such exotic birds as Lockheed Constellations and Boeing Stratocruisers to the skies above my family home. In 1959 the NWRCC regulars in the village included lowbridge Bristol K5Gs and Leyland PD2/21 Titans on the two-hourly service 36 from Northwich to Altrincham and Manchester, and Bristol L5G saloons on short-workings to Pickmere Lake. All of the K5Gs and some of the L5Gs were pre-war chassis which had received new bodywork in the early 1950s, a secret confided to me in hushed tones by a conductor who clearly regarded such shenanigans as an inferior alternative to the purchase of brand-new buses.

In the summer of 1959 I saw my first 'Black Top' Reliance/Willowbrook dual-purpose vehicle. Bowyers had finished and my gran's regular driver from that company, a Mr Prince, had taken up employment with North Western. The Wincham village outings followed him and the 'Black Top' (sadly unidentifiable) was our mount for a private-hire to see Caernarvon Castle and Snowdonia. The 'Box Brownie' recorded its arrival in Caernarvon (as it was then spelt) and accidentally included the front end of a very odd looking double-decker with the registration mark TF 6821. Years would pass before I managed to learn the history of this strange vehicle.

My parents, who up until then had seldom been to anywhere except Blackpool, were apparently impressed with North Wales. Perhaps the trip had reminded them of their honeymoon in 1952 which had been spent at the wonderfully romantic location of the Butlin's camp in Pwllheli. Whatever the reason, our 1960 family holiday took us to Pwllheli, albeit to a boarding-house rather than to Billy Butlin's local stalag of fun.

By then I was seven years old and armed with a notebook and pen. And there was that odd double-decker again, apparently a Leyland, carrying 'Clynnog & Trevor' titles, and about to return to Caernarvon. I noted its registration mark and that of the vehicle behind it, a Crossley double-decker the likes of which had never been seen in Wincham. Over the next seven days I took note of further 'C&T' vehicles, including a pair of Guy Arab double-deckers, and dozens of coaches belonging to other operators. Among the latter was JX 9735, a fully-fronted Leyland Tiger of local business Caelloi Motors. I decided that I liked North Wales.

Family holidays in Rhyl (1961) and Llandudno (1963) followed, separated by a year back in Blackpool, and were slightly disappointing by comparison to the Pwllheli trip. There were still plenty of exotic coaches to record – including Midland Red examples in Llandudno, the first I had ever seen - but all of the stage carriage services were operated by Crosville, a company I was already familiar with from its English operations and had never really taken to. I summoned up the courage to ask a Crosville driver if there were any other bus companies, and if so where could I find them? He grinned, pointed westwards, and said 'Bangor'.

Two years after the Llandudno holiday I was considered old enough to go out for the day on my own. I had heard good things about Wrexham and made several expeditions to the inland Denbighshire town via connections at Northwich and Chester. The main attraction on my first visit was Wright's Wulfrunian, and I rode on this beast up to Rhosllanerchrugog, returning on Williams' almost equally famous Regal IV bus. The next destination on my list was Bangor. It proved to be more difficult to reach than I had thought (readers of my last book will remember that I was a dogmatic little so-and-so at that age and refused to go bus-spotting by train). Since 1962 I had been living in Sale, on the outskirts of Manchester, and in April 1966 an opportunity finally presented itself when North Western subsidiary Altrincham Coachways offered an excursion to both Bangor and Caernarvon.

At 8.30 am on a wet Saturday I boarded SB/ Bella Vega AJA 987B and headed westwards, the only passenger of less than retirement age. The excursion was under-subscribed with only 25 on board so I hid at the back to avoid constant offers of sweets and biscuits. Coachways' schedule featured two hours in Bangor followed by three in Caernarvon. En route to Bangor we passed a rare Seddon Mk 17 service bus, TDM 855, operating a stage route for Phillips of Holywell. It was a good omen. The rest of the day saw vehicles belonging to Deiniolen Motors and Purple of Bethesda entering my notebook in Bangor, while Caernarvon brought machines belonging to Express Motors, Silver Star, and Whiteway, as well as more examples of the Clynnog & Trevor fleet.

An Apology To The Welsh

My grandmother on my father's side of the family, Irene Jones, was born in Flint, making me a quarter Welsh, but her family moved to St Helens in Lancashire when she was a baby and she never became fluent in the Welsh language. I speak none, and I am now too old to learn. Those who doubt this should hear me attempt to pronounce the word 'Caelloi' (Kerthloy??) despite repeated attempts at tuition by my good friend David Thomas at the Manchester Museum of Transport. I hope that Welsh readers will forgive me for this as I have nothing but admiration for their ancient culture and language.

Another thing which may require an apology is my use of 'pre-1970s' spellings for place names (eg Caernarvon rather than Caernarfon, Trevor instead of Trefor). No insult is intended as the older spellings are those which appear repeatedly in the photographic content, and it would seem peculiar to present the more modern (and culturally respectful) versions in the accompanying text.

As with the two previous volumes in this series on independent bus operators (covering Staffordshire and Shropshire) the pre-1974 county boundaries are observed throughout so chapters carry the titles 'Caernarvonshire & Anglesey' rather than Gwynedd, and 'Denbighshire & Flintshire' rather than Clwyd.

The low population density of North Wales (apart from the coastal strip and the Dee valley) has been a constant problem for those seeking to operate economically viable stage carriage services in the region. Given these harsh realities it is gratifying (and slightly astounding) that one of the operators covered in this book is celebrating a landmark anniversary in the springtime of 2012. The Clynnog & Trefor Motor Company (to use the current version of its name) will be 100 years old and is still operating its original service from Caernarvon to Pwllheli. A second North Wales company, Caelloi of Pwllheli, is celebrating its 90th year as an operator of motorised buses/ coaches in 2012, a distinction made necessary by the fact that the business was originally a traditional village carrier and can trace the 'horse-drawn' part of its history back to 1851. The company's original stage service from Dinas to Pwllheli was abandoned at deregulation and most of Caelloi's current revenue is derived from extended coach tours.

Another pioneering operator, Express Motors (founded in 1908) is also still in existence. Its original service from Cesarea (now known as Y Fron) to Caernarvon passed to local rival Silver Star more than 40 years ago but the company continued as a coach operator and after deregulation became active in bidding for tendered local bus services across a large part of Gwynedd. Silver Star itself is another proud survivor, but as with Caelloi is now primarily a coach operator. Its stage services, which commenced in 1920, were recently put up for sale and (ironically) passed to Express Motors, including that company's original route.

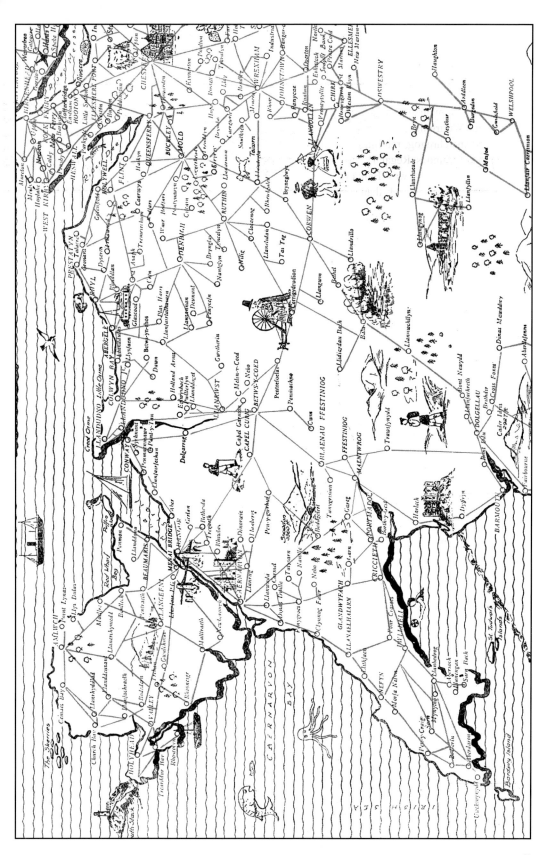

5

As a perusal of the various operator histories in this book will rapidly confirm, these are by no means the only survivors from the pioneering days of the industry. Despite the best efforts of enormous and well-financed intruders such as the Great Western Railway, Crosville, and the post-deregulation conglomerates, the locally owned independent bus industry is alive and well in North Wales. To understand why this is so, when so many areas of the UK have been thoroughly monopolised, we need to go back in time to the earliest years of the last century and (briefly) beyond.

From The Romans
To The Railways

For almost 2000 years the northern part of Wales has been invaded by foreign forces intent upon the seizure of its valuable natural resources, although in fairness it should be stated that the Welsh themselves represented an earlier invasion of the area. The Cymri, a Celtic tribe from mainland Europe, arrived in Wales between 500 and 400 BC, displacing or assimilating the previous inhabitants, but they differed from subsequent newcomers in seeing the country as somewhere to settle rather than merely to exploit and then disappear with the booty like thieves in the night.

The Romans arrived in the first century of the current era, their incursion motivated by reports of extensive gold deposits in the Welsh mountain ranges. Once the mining operations were established they tended to leave the local inhabitants to go about their own business – unless that business included a desire to repel the foreigners or to interrupt the extraction of stolen treasure.

In less than 400 years the great Roman Empire disintegrated and the Welsh looked forward to a better future. It was not to be. The news that Britain was no longer defended by the empire spread like wildfire among the Anglo-Saxon tribes of northern Germany and a new invasion of the eastern seaboard soon began. By 600 AD the country now known as England was in the hands of the new invaders, and tens of thousands of refugees from the 'Romano-British' tribes had fled westwards to join their Celtic cousins or had been pushed northwards into Scotland.

Attempts by the Anglo-Saxon newcomers to take control of Wales by 'divide and rule' tactics were never entirely successful (more so in the south of the country than in the north), and the would-be invaders peevishly decided that Wales was more trouble than it was worth. The Anglo-Saxon Kingdom of Mercia built Offa's Dyke as an easily defended frontier between themselves and the unconquered Welsh tribes.

Even then there was little peace in the area as Viking raiders entered the picture around 800 AD and were to plague the Welsh for almost two centuries from their base across the Irish Sea in Dublin. And then, in 1066, the forces of the Duchy of Normandy (itself a Viking colony in France) landed on the south coast of England under the leadership of the man known as 'William the Bastard'. His success against the English earned him the more acceptable nickname of 'William the Conqueror'.

After the death of Harold, the Anglo-Saxon King, English territory fell to the Normans at an astonishing rate as the surviving aristocrats fled or became traitors. The next item on the 'Conqueror's' shopping list was Welsh gold. To cut a long and painful story short, Wales finally fell to the English crown at the end of the 13th century. As the supply of gold began to dwindle the new invaders turned to other valuable commodities such as stone, slate, copper, tin, iron, and coal. Bleeding heart liberals who bemoan British exploitation of Ireland, or of colonies on other continents, tend to forget that the Welsh were the first to suffer from the rapacity of English imperial avarice.

The crimes against the Welsh were not limited to robbery and political repression. A deliberate attempt was made over many centuries to eradicate the Welsh language and to belittle and eliminate the nation's cultural traditions. In Victorian times some English aristocrats who had already prospered from the theft of Welsh natural resources turned their attention to the burgeoning tourist industry (promoted by the development of the railway system) and turned small coastal villages such as Rhyl and Colwyn Bay into large resort towns which catered almost entirely for English visitors. Further west in Llandudno the Pryce-Lloyd family, Welsh in its blood but English in its loyalties, took the leading role in developing the largest of all the resorts. The North Wales coast became the Benidorm of its day, with most of the profits being transported across the border as surely as the gold of an earlier time.

The first motor-buses to be employed on stage carriage services in northwestern Wales were these two Swiss-made Orions with Dodson bodywork, CC 162 and CC 163, the Cambrian Railways' fleet numbers 1 and 2. The pair entered service on the route from the Nevin area to Pwllheli in June 1906, but the Orion engines were less reliable than had been hoped. In 1912 the bodywork from the two vehicles was transferred to two second-hand Milnes Daimler chassis which also inherited the Orions' registration marks. It was hardly worth the effort as the Cambrian withdrew from the route in February 1913. *(ME Jones Collection)*

As can be seen, Traffic lorry-bus CC 2029 was little more than a flatbed with benches attached like many of its contemporaries. The vehicle was operated by WJ Jones of Bottwnog, trading as Talafon Motors, and was used on a Wednesday and Saturday stage route from Pwllheli to Rhiw, at the western end of the Lleyn peninsula, in the early 1920s. Talafon was acquired by Crosville ten years later. *(ME Jones Collection)*

On the original postcard from which this image is taken the sub-title reads 'The First Motor Bus in Abersoch'. It may well have been, but the suspicion must be that the view was taken in the West Riding of Yorkshire rather than on the Lleyn peninsula, as the Karrier (made in Huddersfield) was still carrying its manufacturer's trade-plate CX 0418. After delivery in April 1912 it became CC 540 with the Abersoch Motor Omnibus Co. *(ME Jones Collection)*

This widely known postcard view shows the 'Karrier Trio' at Pwllheli in the spring of 1912. From left to right the vehicles are CC 540 of the Abersoch company, CC 547 of Nevin Green, and CC 524 of Tocia. Thanks to the late John Dunabin's excellent book covering Tocia and its rivals, it can be recorded that the two outer vehicles are on B80 chassis and have 32-seat bodies built by Stagg & Robson. Such details are unavailable for CC 547 with its distinctly different radiator and bodywork. *(ME Jones Collection)*

As in colonial India, all of this exploitation did have one positive aspect for the inhabitants of North Wales – an extensive railway network which connected all corners of the 'principality' to the outside world. Dozens of small railway companies were established and inevitably some of them were little better than scams designed to separate investors from their money. In the crisis that followed the end of the railway boom many of the companies serving Wales were forced to amalgamate to survive, resulting in the formation of the Cambrian Railways – despite its name based in Oswestry, across the border in Shropshire. Times were still hard, and in 1905 the directors of the Cambrian, reluctant to develop new lines on routes of questionable profitability, decided to experiment with motor-buses.

The Railway Pioneers

The Cambrian was not quite the first. In October 1904 the Great Western Railway had opened a bus service from its railhead at Wrexham to Holt and Farndon, using double-deck Milnes-Daimler vehicles. As this experiment was taking place less than 12 miles from the Cambrian's headquarters it can be safely assumed that the Oswestry-based company's directors were taking notice.

Within a year the Cambrian had bought two Swiss-built Orion buses fitted with 22-seat Dodson bodywork, and on 18th June 1906 opened a route from their railhead at Pwllheli to Nevin and Edeyrn on the north coast of the Lleyn peninsula. The Orions proved to be of dubious reliability but remained in service for six years. Plans to extend the bus network were, however, quietly abandoned.

A less modest example of railway involvement in the story of North Wales' bus services emerged in 1910 when the London & North Western Railway (LNWR) began a service from Connah's Quay to Mold and Flint. Another major LNWR bus route, from their station at Colwyn Bay to the neighbouring resort of Rhos-on-Sea, commenced in 1914. This was operated by, among other vehicles, a Leyland 'torpedo' char-a-banc which has now been restored to its original condition by the well-known preservationist Mike Sutcliffe.

In 1912 the Cambrian finally admitted that the Orions were unfit for purpose and transferred their Dodson bodies to two Milnes-Daimler chassis

acquired from the London General Omnibus Co. This cheapskate manoeuvre failed to impress the travelling public and in February 1913 the railway abandoned its bus operations, advising its passengers to use the services of a local company known as Nevin Green.

In the mid-1920s the Great Western Railway, having swallowed up the Cambrian Railways group in 1922, started to expand its bus operations in North Wales, responding to increasing competition from (and abstraction of traffic by) the growing bus industry in the region. By 1925 the GWR had opened new routes from Wrexham to Brymbo and Rhosllanerchrugog, and from Oswestry to Llangollen, the Tanat valley, and Welshpool, using a varied fleet of AEC, Burford, Guy, Maudslay, and Thornycroft manufacture. In the same year the GWR established a bus outpost in Caernarvonshire by acquiring Nevin Green, bringing the Pwllheli to Nevin and Edeyrn service back into railway ownership.

Trailblazing Independents

Mention has already been made of some of Caernarvonshire's earliest independents including Express Motors (founded in 1908) and Clynnog & Trevor (1912) but there were dozens of other locally owned operators which failed to achieve their longevity. The more significant ones such as Richardson's Busy Bee, Caernarvon Bay Motors, and the Seiont and Tocia companies, are reasonably well-known to transport historians, but there were also many 'one man bands' with an equally fascinating tale to tell.

My personal favourite among these was known as the Nantile Vale Star Motor Bus Service (six words in its title, one vehicle in its inventory) which commenced operations from its home village to Caernarvon in 1919. Its only bus was a Ford Model T equipped with bodywork by a local craftsman. Passengers referred to the vehicle as 'The House on Wheels' which might suggest a rather clumsy appearance.

Rural roads were (and still are) rarely illuminated by street lighting and on a particularly dark night in 1927 'The House on Wheels' collided with a stray cow and the vehicle's bodywork completely disintegrated. Miraculously, all of its occupants survived, as did the cow, but the home-made vehicle itself was uninsured against collision with livestock and the company ceased to trade. Its service was taken over by the Seiont company and ultimately passed to Crosville.

While most of the independent operations in rural Caernarvonshire were owned by local proprietors, those active in the well-populated coastal resorts were as likely to be the property of English financiers as the resorts themselves. A&R Motors (which operated from Pwllheli to Portmadoc) was a subsidiary of Avery & Roberts, a Liverpool coaching agency. The company's prime mover, Gustav Roberts, also had shares in another North Wales operator, Bangor Blue, and in Lancashire United Transport.

Across the Menai Strait in Anglesey the two leading independents of the day were Holyhead Motors (trading as 'Mona Maroon' and a subsidiary of the London-financed Seaside Resorts & Development Co) and UNU Motor Services. The 'UNU' of the title allegedly stood for 'U Need Us' and the company was owned by the Lancashire coach operator William Webster of Wigan.

Back in Caernarvonshire, but further to the east, the largest locally based operator was the Llandudno Coaching & Carriage Company. This business had been founded in 1897 by two English businessmen, George Woodyatt and John James, and in 1902 had opened a large livery stables at the junction of Queens Road and Curzon Road. The company later acquired a fleet of char-a-bancs for excursion work and this aspect of the company was marketed as Royal Blue Motors. Stage carriage services inevitably followed after the end of the First World War and the bus fleet had grown to include more than 50 vehicles by 1923. At this point the two founders decided that more capital was needed and a controlling interest was sold to the (London-based) BAT subsidiary of British Electric Traction. One side effect of this transaction was the appearance in the 'Royal Blue' fleet of a large number of SOS vehicles built by Midland Red. The relationship between the two BET group companies had further 'synergy' (as modern yuppies might say) as Midland Red operated express coach services to Llandudno from both Birmingham and London.

Moving eastwards into Denbighshire the major resort of Colwyn Bay was served by 'Royal Blue' and another prominent Llandudno-based operator, North Wales Silver Motors. This company was backed by indigenous investors and found capital for expansion harder to come by than its rival. As a result its fleet peaked at 26 vehicles, less than a third of the number then operated by the BET sponsored 'Royal Blue'. The lack of a resident operator in Colwyn Bay was partially explained by the existence of the Llandudno & Colwyn Bay Electric Railway's coastal tramway. The tramway company would later purchase a stake in North Wales Silver Motors and use its buses to replace a section of its track which had proven to be unprofitable.

In the 'pre-Clwyd' days the Denbighshire coastal strip was relatively narrow and the next large resort town, Rhyl, was in the county of Flintshire. As I explained in my earlier book on Shropshire independents, Flintshire was an entirely artificial creation consisting of two unconnected territories and ruled for many centuries from Chester as a 'buffer state' between England and Wales. In the coastal part of the county the largest independent operator by far was Brookes Brothers, based in Rhyl, which traded as 'White Rose Motor Buses'.

Joseph and Daniel Brookes had started operating char-a-banc excursions in 1912 and were also involved in removals and general haulage. Local bus services began just before the outbreak of the First World War and by 1916 double-deckers were in use. The company became the most important independent operator in North Wales with almost 100 buses and coaches. While few pre-1939 independents have much of a memorial to their existence beyond a handful of old photographs and the written word, Brookes Brothers is a notable exception. Two of the company's original vehicles are still roadworthy in the hands of talented preservationists, the site of the main depot is now a shopping precinct known as 'The White Rose Centre', and an extensive Brookes Brothers archive collected by a local enthusiast recently passed into the ownership of The Omnibus Society for a staggering £2,800.

Turning inland an enthusiast of the post-1945 era could not fail to notice the immaculately presented cream and red double-deckers of Pryce and Owen Lloyd of Bagillt. These vehicles (which included a Foden PVD6, two Guy Arab IVs, and a PD3 Titan, all bought when brand-new) were, despite their smart appearance, used exclusively on works services to local steel and textile industry sites. The company is still active

The Clynnog & Trevor Motor Company's very first bus was this 35-seat Commer WP, CC 553, delivered to the firm in July 1912. It gave a full ten years of service on the Caernarvon to Pwllheli route, an exceptionally long life-span for a vehicle of its time. *(Clynnog & Trevor Motor Co)*

In the mid-1920s Clynnog & Trevor switched their allegiance from Commer to Karrier, bringing them into line with their fellow independents further to the west. CC 6504 was a 26-seat Karrier CL4, bought new in June 1926. Later Karriers such as this one proved to be less robust than some of their predecessors, and the vehicle was withdrawn during 1934 after eight years with C&T. *(Clynnog & Trevor Motor Co)*

These three vehicles are in Caernarvon in the early 1920s. The one on the left remains unidentified, but the other two are B 2408 (centre) and B 2409 (right), Leylands of Richards' Busy Bee company. Both had gone by 1925 when Richards sold out to Crosville. The route board on B 2408 is for the service to Ebenezer, a community soon to be renamed as Deiniolen, while that on B 2409 is for the long and wild service to Beddgelert. *(ME Jones Collection)*

This unidentified Lancia belonged to OR Williams & Sons of Waenfawr – then trading as Caernarvon & Waenfawr District Motors, but later to become better known as Whiteway. Busy Bee's B 2409 (see above) would have passed the Williams garage on its way to Beddgelert. *(C Carter via Peter Harden)*

and after deregulation became involved in local bus services for the first time in more than 60 years.

Phillips of Holywell (founded just after the First World War) is another survivor from the early days of the stage carriage motor-bus industry, and prospered thanks to a licence for an important and well-patronised route from Holywell to Mold. It also bought a brand-new Foden PVD6 double-decker, identical to Lloyd's example, plus many other second-hand double-deckers and a succession of new Seddon saloons.

To reach the other ('detached') part of Flintshire the traveller had to return into Denbighshire or cross the English border and pass through western Cheshire. The southern portion of Flintshire had no towns but contained one village of great significance to the local bus industry. The Chesworth family's 'Pioneer Motor Services', based in Bronington, had every right to use the name as its services began to operate in 1908. Most of its stage carriage mileage was across the border in Shropshire with a 'hub' at Whitchurch, and the company's network was eventually sold to Salopia Saloon Coaches, based in that town.

From 1920 the Chesworths had local competition from William Fisher, also of Bronington and destined to outlast the 'Pioneer' by more than four decades. Most of Fisher's routes ran to Oswestry or Whitchurch (both in Shropshire) or to Chester. A logical extension in the direction of Wrexham, which would have provided Fisher with a Welsh connection, was pre-empted by the presence of other operators with deeper pockets – operators which were best left alone in the hope that they might not notice a modest operation at the fringe of their sphere of influence.

Wrexham was surrounded by major coalfields and grew to a point where it merited a street tramway, operated by a subsidiary of British Electric Traction. The trams, however, were noted for their aversion to hills and many of the largest mining villages were left unconnected to the tramway system. Wrexham & District (the tramway operator) was slow to develop motor-bus services to such communities and the vacuum was enthusiastically filled by a swarm of tiny independents, most of them 'one man band' entrepreneurs who had returned from the battlefields of the First World War with the ability to drive and sufficient capital to purchase a taxi.

Although largely unscheduled and operating initially with car-sized vehicles, their shared taxi services were economical to use as they would wait until the vehicle was full of passengers before departing for the town centre or one of the local collieries. Their popularity survived Wrexham & District's belated attempts to compete, as the tramway operator was perceived as an 'English' company (due to its ownership by BET) and most villagers chose to support local businesses whenever possible. The bus operations of the Great Western Railway were similarly viewed and many passengers preferred to wait in the rain for locally owned vehicles to arrive rather than patronise the fleet of the GWR.

By 1930 more than two dozen of the former taxi operators had graduated to larger vehicles, ranging from 14-seaters up to full-size 32-seat saloons, and were subsequently licensed by the North West Traffic Commissioners at the beginning of the regulated era. The small companies established a branch of the United Bus Owners' Association to represent their common interests, and the Wrexham branch was still active in the 1960s long after the rest of the UBOA had ceased to exist. This solidarity helped to ensure their survival as independents across the North Wales region found themselves at war with the monopolistic might of 'The Combine'.

The Elephant In The Room

There was a curious form of voluntary public transport apartheid in Wrexham which survived well into the 1970s. People who lived in (majority) English speaking areas, such as the town itself and the valley heading southwards, had no aversion to the English owned buses of Wrexham & District, the GWR, or their successor companies. Those who lived in the (majority) Welsh speaking mining villages preferred to avoid them. This was far more than economic xenophobia. Few who travelled regularly outside of the Wrexham area could have failed to notice the rapid advance of another English company, snuffing out local businesses like the sparks of human souls as it moved relentlessly westwards.

The Crosville Motor Company had its headquarters in Chester, in earlier times the base for Roman legions and other unwelcome intruders, and its owners – the Taylor family – were the descendants of a wealthy Yorkshire mill-owner. George Crosland Taylor (1858-1923) showed little interest in his father's Worsted Coating Mill in Huddersfield and headed across the Pennines into Cheshire to develop his own empire. He was particularly fond of the 'new technology' industries of his day and in 1882 founded GC Taylor & Co to manufacture electrical cables at Neston on the Wirral peninsula. This business would merge with others over the years to become BICC, an industrial giant of the 20th century. Much of the Taylor company's trade (and its proprietor's snowballing fortune) came from supplying cables to the tramway operators of South Lancashire and North Wales.

Crosland Taylor (he chose to use his second 'Christian' name which honoured his mother's family) had no interest in tramways except as a source of orders for his company's products. He preferred vehicles powered by internal combustion engines, and from 1903 onwards made an annual pilgrimage to Paris to attend the motor show held in the French capital. At the 1905 event he met Georges de Ville, a car designer working for the Morane company, and the two men agreed that Taylor would form a business to licence-produce de Ville's designs for the British market.

In the following year Taylor imported a 'starter package' made up of two completed cars, the chassis of a third, and the blueprints to produce more. The Crosville Motor Company, founded at Crane Wharf, Chester, in October 1906, took its title from the 'Christian' name of its English co-proprietor and the surname of the French designer, although de Ville had no actual shareholding in the firm. Crosland Taylor's partner in the new enterprise was Charles William Catt, a businessman from Belper in Derbyshire, who shared his enthusiasm for motor-cars and took a 32% interest in Crosville. Taylor held 64% with the remainder in the hands of a senior employee. This position changed in June 1907 when Catt increased his share to almost equal that of Crosland Taylor and his family.

Despite the best efforts of its co-proprietors, by 1908 it had become clear that Crosville would never be successful as a motor manufacturer. Only a handful of cars had been sold in the first two years, and three of those had been manufactured in France and merely badged in Chester. The company survived by doing repair work, offering car-hire services, and teaching people how to drive. CW Catt and his kindred lost interest and had reduced their shareholding to zero by September 1910.

In their place came the Yorkshireman's three sons. The eldest, Edward Crosland Taylor, became Crosville's general manager in June 1909 and a director in September 1910. Six months later he decided to emigrate to the United States, but despite his brief involvement in the company he made one decision which proved to be crucial to its future prosperity. On a visit to an auction in Swansea, ostensibly to buy second-hand cars, he was tempted by a Herald char-a-banc (registered in Glamorgan as L 517), paid the 'bargain' asking price, and brought it back to Chester. Crosville had entered the bus industry.

The Herald was never that reliable (thus the 'bargain') and several other char-a-bancs soon entered the fleet to cover for its spasmodic serviceability. At around that time a local entrepreneur had just started a stage carriage service to Chester from Kelsall and was clearly doing well, so the Taylors began to make plans for their own scheduled operation of a route from Chester to Ellesmere Port on the Mersey estuary. Various licensing difficulties delayed the first service on this route which eventually started in February 1911.

Edward left the country shortly afterwards and was replaced on the Crosville board by his younger brother, Claude Crosland Taylor. It should perhaps be explained that George Crosland Taylor gave all of his sons the final 'Christian' name of Crosland, either as a gross act of egotism or in an attempt to make them sound 'double-barrelled' to the Cheshire aristocracy of their new social milieu. It goes without saying that such a ploy was doomed to fail and would mark the Taylors out as irretrievably gauche to the hardened snobs of the 'old money' crowd.

The Ellesmere Port service was a resounding success, and the company subsequently bought the route which had inspired it, from Chester to Kelsall. A second base of operations was established at Crewe in 1913 and Crosville began to acquire other operators to establish a near monopoly in western Cheshire. Initial expansion was slow due to the onset of the First World War but accelerated to a headlong speed after the Armistice. In 1919 Crosville started its first

This old postcard image is sub-titled 'Bangor Blue Motors January 1921'. In real life this 14-seat Ford Model T was actually delivered in November 1922 and this view is more likely to have been taken at the end of the company's existence rather than at its beginning. Evidence for this is provided by the vehicles in the background which include Bangor Blue Dennis E CC 7116 (delivered in June 1927) and Royal Blue SOS QL type CC 7742 (new in 1928). *(Author's Collection)*

The 1929/30 winter timetable of Rhiwen Motors. Rhiwen was the original trading name of JW Hughes & Son of Deiniolen. After selling the lion's share of the business to Crosville the Hughes family continued to trade as Deiniolen Motors. *(Author's Collection)*

RHIWEN MOTORS WINTER 1929-30 TIME TABLE.

Rhiwlas, Caerhun & Bangor Route.

WEEK DAYS.					SATURDAYS.							

Proprietors: J. W. HUGHES & SON, Rhiwen Garage, Deiniolen.

Special Bus leaves Bangor every Wednesday at 1 p.m., 8.15 p.m. and 10 p.m.

An unidentified Leyland char-a-banc of the Penmaenmawr Motor Co, circa 1925. The building visible on the right hand side is thought to be the cafe at Fairy Glen. Several versions of this print are known to exist (one can be found online) and the postcard example used here is unhelpfully sub-titled 'A Day out on a Chara'. Another postcard using the same photograph claims that the vehicle is on its way to Blackpool – unlikely given the 12 mph speed limit displayed on its skirt panels. *(ME Jones Collection)*

North Wales Silver Motors bought this 32-seat Dennis bus, CC 1807, in 1921, and it was still in the fleet when Crosville bought the company in August 1930. Crosville gave it the fleet number 115 but only kept it until the following year. *(Peter Harden Collection)*

service across the border into Wales, a circular route from Chester to Mold and Flint.

For most of the next three years Crosville turned its attention to southwest Lancashire and the lucrative territory to the north of the Mersey which included Warrington and Widnes, but in 1922 they acquired their first Welsh operator. Roberts of Llanrwst (trading as Blue Motors) was a modest enough purchase which brought a Bettws-y-Coed to Abergele route and a single Leyland GH into the Crosville fold. Further expansion was temporarily delayed by the death of the founder in 1923, but before too long Claude Crosland Taylor (and his younger brother Winthrop James Crosland Taylor who had joined the firm in 1918) were back on the take-over trail and moving into Caernarvonshire.

In November 1925 they bought the business of Richards (Busy Bee) of Caernarvon, bringing services from Caernarvon to Beddgelert, Portmadoc, and Pwllheli, two AECs and two Lancias into Crosville ownership. The company had already established new bases at Dolgellau and Blaenau Festiniog in the previous year and Richards' premises became the third Crosville depot in the western part of North Wales. It was only the beginning. Between October 1927 and October 1928 the company acquired the previously mentioned A&R Motors of Criccieth and three smaller Caernarvonshire operators including Peris Motors of Llanberis.

At that point North Wales was a patchwork quilt of medium-sized bus operators. Heading westwards from Chester, Crosville was the most significant operator in northern Flintshire but was denied the prize of Rhyl by the local fleet of Brookes Brothers (White Rose). The coastal region of Denbighshire, including the major resort of Colwyn Bay, was dominated by the local tramway company and operators from Llandudno including 'Royal Blue' and North Wales Silver Motors. In 1928 'Royal Blue' had extended its territory westwards from Llandudno by acquiring Bangor Blue from Gustav Roberts. In northern Caernarvonshire Crosville held sway over many of the trunk inter-urban routes, but had barely made an impact in the rural inland areas which were still in the hands of small independents, while Anglesey was still dominated by two medium-sized (and English owned) operators, Mona Maroon and UNU.

All of that was about to change. In 1928 the four mainline railway companies had finally obtained powers to operate bus services after a four year battle. Although the GWR had been operating bus routes in Wales (and elsewhere) since 1904, most railway bus services in existence before 1928 had existed in a precarious legal limbo. The corporate ancestors of the 'Big Four' railway companies had been established by individual Acts of Parliament which narrowly defined the legitimate business of such enterprises. As the motor-bus industry had not yet come into existence at the time of these Acts, local bus services were obviously not included in these definitions.

All railway-operated bus routes started before 1928 (with the exception of some GWR services which had already been empowered by secondary legislation) had been justified by sections of the various Acts which allowed the railway companies to offer connecting road services between railway stations and communities not yet served by railway lines. While this loophole, originally intended for horse-drawn vehicles, easily admitted the LNWR (later LMSR)'s operations in North Wales, it seemed to exclude any larger scale possibilities. Even the GWR, which had a wider remit in its Parliamentary Acts, was reluctant to invest beyond a certain point until the ambiguity was resolved.

By 1924 the mainline railways had undoubtedly lost some of their local traffic to bus operators, and the 'Big Four' (GWR, LMSR, LNER, and SR) had started a political campaign to be allowed to operate bus services in competition with their new trackless rivals. The political lobbying was intense and was undoubtedly assisted by the fact that most MPs were wealthy men with investment portfolios which included railway company shares. Very few of them were financially connected to the bus industry.

The two largest bus-operating conglomerates, British Electric Traction and Thomas Tilling, decided to abandon their opposition to the railways in exchange for a mutually advantageous deal. Aware that the railway companies preferred to negotiate with a single entity the two holding companies established a new joint venture, Tilling & British Automobile Traction (T&BAT) to control most of their bus-operating subsidiaries. T&BAT then offered 50% of the shares in each subsidiary to the appropriate railway company (or companies) which covered the same geographical area.

In light of modern anti-monopoly legislation it can be difficult to imagine such a deal. The four mainline railway companies already shared an almost complete 'tetrapoly' of British passenger train services. The treaty with T&BAT to create the monstrosity popularly known as 'The Combine' gave them most of the country's inter-urban bus services, and they went on (via Railway Air Services) to control most of the nation's domestic air routes. At the time all of this was legal whereas today it would be seen as criminal collusion wilfully intended to suppress competition.

Some areas of the country remained stubbornly disorganised, North Wales among them, due to the absence of an existing Tilling or BET group stranglehold upon local bus operations. The dominant railway companies in North Wales, the GWR and the LMSR, set out to rectify this situation. On 1st May 1929 the Taylor family sold the Crosville Motor Company to the LMSR for just under £400,000 – the equivalent of £20 million today. The two Taylor brothers remained at the helm, having received the LMSR board's endorsement as two ruthless and carnivorous young men very much to their liking.

The combination of the Taylors' acquisitive nature and the railway companys' almost bottomless pockets became an irresistible force to many bus operators in North Wales. In October 1929, to accentuate the change of ownership, the Crosville Motor Company was placed into liquidation and replaced by a new entity known as LMS (Crosville). On 4th November 1929 the LMS acquired Mona Maroon, and two months later UNU, giving the railway company a near monopoly in Anglesey. In February 1930 Brookes Brothers (White Rose of Rhyl) fell into LMS ownership although the Brookes family retained the removals and haulage part of their company. By the first anniversary of its acquisition of Crosville, the LMSR considered its house to be sufficiently in order to place its North Wales bus assets into 'The Combine'.

On 1st May 1930 LMS (Crosville), Mona Maroon with 11 vehicles, UNU with 22 vehicles, and Brookes Brothers with 87, were merged into a new company, Crosville Motor Services Ltd, with the Taylor brothers still employed as its senior executives. On the same day the LMSR sold 50%

of its shares in the new company to T&BAT to create a typical 'Combine' ownership structure. Six months later the T&BAT-controlled Wrexham & District company (which had abandoned its tramway in 1927) was merged with the GWR's bus network in North Wales, the new operator becoming known as Western Transport and featuring a similar 50/50 ownership split between T&BAT and 'God's Wonderful Railway'.

The hectic pace of change continued as 'The Combine' tightened its grip on the nation's bus services. Red Dragon of Denbigh was acquired by Crosville in July 1930, North Wales Silver Motors of Llandudno (with 26 vehicles) in August, and Llangoed Red of Anglesey in October. In February 1931 T&BAT sold its Llandudno Coaching & Carriage Company affiliate ('Royal Blue') to Crosville along with 80 vehicles. January 1932 saw Crosville acquiring Bethesda Greys and a major part of the JW Hughes business of Deiniolen, while December 1932 brought Caernarvon Bay Motors into Crosville ownership. The biggest acquisition of them all came on 1st May 1933 when Crosville absorbed Western Transport with 133 vehicles and services extending from Wrexham to Machynlleth and Pwllheli. In line with the 'Combine' agreement the GWR received half of the LMSR's 50% shareholding in Crosville in exchange for its shares in Western Transport.

Famous names continued to disappear at an alarming rate in 1934/5, some of them pioneers from the earliest days of the bus industry. The Lleyn peninsula in western Caernarvonshire was a particular target and the businesses acquired there included Nevin Blue, Williams of Mynytho, Tocia of Aberdaron (with its origins in a horse-drawn service which started in 1860), Jones (Talafon Motors) of Bottwnog, Roberts of Rhoshirwaen, Owen of Dinas, and Evans of Llithfaen. Anglesey was also 'tidied up' by the purchase of five smaller operators, and Crosville's (ex-Western Transport) presence in Wrexham enlarged still further by the acquisition of Rothwell of Holt, Price of Wrexham, and the stage carriage services of Mates of Chirk. Other significant acquisitions over the two year period were of the Seiont Motor Bus Co of Caernarvon (in June 1934) and New Blue Motors of Llandudno Junction (in April 1935).

And it didn't end there. In 1936 Crosville acquired 10 more North Wales independents including Roberts of Southsea (near Wrexham)

Royal Blue of Llandudno also liked Dennises and this two and a half ton variant, CC 3701, was delivered to them in 1923. This particular machine had already been withdrawn by the time of the Crosville take-over in 1931, but several others from the same batch were included in the deal. *(Peter Harden Collection)*

Brookes Brothers (White Rose) of Rhyl was taken over by Crosville in 1930. This Leyland SG7 with 44-seat dual doorway bodywork, also by Leyland, was delivered to the Rhyl operator in 1923 as fleet number 27. DM 2583 was allocated the Crosville fleet number 440 but was withdrawn from use in 1931. For decades afterwards it served as a static caravan on a farm before being rescued and fully restored by the famous preservationist Mike Sutcliffe. *(Author's Collection)*

Edward Henry Phillips started his eponymous bus company in Holywell with a converted car and three converted Sunbeam ambulances. Stage carriage services demanded something with more credibility and resulted in the acquisition of this 30 cwt Dennis, DM 5170, in 1927. The vehicle is operating on the main service to Mold. *(Author's Collection)*

The London & North Western Railway had several bus routes in North Wales, including feeder services from Holywell to Holywell Station, and from Rhos-on-Sea to Colwyn Bay Station. Their most ambitious operation in the region connected the Flintshire towns of Connah's Quay, Flint, Northop, and Mold and merited double-deck equipment. This unidentified L&NWR Milnes-Daimler appears to have been posed for some kind of official photograph, but no details are given on the postcard original. *(ME Jones Collection)*

with eight vehicles and DM Motors of Llanrug (near Caernarvon) with 10. By comparison the three year period from 1937-9 featured just six acquisitions, possibly because everybody who might be persuaded to sell out had already done so. Four small Wrexham area businesses were acquired in 1940, although three of these operated 7-seat vehicles on the Coedpoeth service having never moved up from large taxis to small buses. The only other wartime purchases were a couple of 'one man bands' taken over in 1941, one in Colwyn Bay, and the other in Anglesey.

In 1942 the alliance between BET and Thomas Tilling ruptured as a result of what divorce lawyers might call 'irreconcilable differences' (a phrase synonymous with 'mutual loathing') and the T&BAT holding company was dissolved. The fact that this event occurred in the middle of the Second World War, when patriotism would normally have demanded stability, shows just how much the relationship between the two companies had deteriorated in the 14 years of 'The Combine's' existence. In the subsequent division of assets T&BAT's 50% shareholdings in bus-operating subsidiaries covered by the 'Combine' agreement were evenly distributed to Tilling and BET on a company-by-company basis. The Tilling group was awarded custody of Crosville which then found itself surrounded by BET companies on every side. Railway shareholdings were unaffected by this corporate schism so Crosville's ownership became divided between Tilling (50%), the LMSR (25%), and the GWR (25%). As a result of this increase in Tilling influence Crosville changed its livery from LMSR maroon to Tilling green and its vehicle choice from Leylands to Bristols. Its acquisitive nature remained unchanged,

Most post-war purchases were of Wrexham area operators, beginning with FW Strange in 1947 and continuing with Williams of Marchwiel in 1951 and Davies Brothers of Summerhill in 1953. An exception to this rule occurred in 1952 when Crosville acquired Ellis Blue Motors of Llanllechid in Caernarvonshire along with a profitable route from Gerlan to Bangor, three Bedfords, a Crossley SD42, and a Guy Vixen. The Crossley coach surprised many observers by remaining in the Crosville fleet for more than five years, an unexpected odd man out among the hordes of identical ECW-bodied Bristols.

The Third Brother

Claude Crosland Taylor died in 1935 and his younger brother took the reins at Crosville. The Taylor dynasty survived, long after the family sold its shareholding, at the behest of the railway companies who owned 50% of Crosville and trusted the Taylors far more than they trusted their 'Combine' allies at T&BAT. In 1939, emboldened perhaps by his recent accession to the throne, Winthrop James Crosland Taylor (known to his friends as Jim) officially changed his name to Winthrop James Crosland-Taylor by 'renouncing his former Christian name of Crosland' and adopting the new double-barrelled surname complete with hyphen. It was a rather strange move so late in life and one never taken by his father or two older brothers.

He went on to write a history of the Crosville company in two parts, 'The Sowing and the Harvest' which covered the years from 1906 until 1948 and 'State Owned Without Tears' which updated the story from the Tilling group's acquisition by the government in 1948 until 1953. Those who consider this present account of the North Wales bus industry too partial to the independents and (heaven forbid!) anti-Crosville in nature may wish to redress the balance by reading Crosland-Taylor's works.

As might be expected he finds little fault in the company founded by his father, and speaks of Crosville's expansion into Wales in much the same tone as Victorian era Americans might have employed while justifying their own murderous expansion westwards. Throughout his books Crosville is portrayed as a naturally superior creature, seizing well-deserved territory from intrinsically inferior local bus operators, or 'pirates' as the Taylors were inclined to describe them. The words 'manifest destiny' are never used but the implications of that arrogant and self-serving doctrine are present throughout his published works.

One particularly telling quotation from 'The Sowing and the Harvest' might serve to illustrate this point. Speaking of rural Wales, away from the English-financed resort towns, he states that '... the bus services are, with few exceptions, pitifully thin, and the houses in villages of any size are ugly and without imagination.' Some might have applied exactly the same adjectives to George

Crosland Taylor himself, a man of 'unfortunate' physical aspect resembling a hybrid between Ebenezer Scrooge and a malevolent goblin, and to his brood of embarrassingly pseudo-eponymous sons.

The independent operators interviewed for this book over the last 25 years were (almost universally) disdainful of the Taylors and the company which they founded. The general feeling was that anybody could have done what they did given enough railway money and a succession of governments with no taste for the preservation of competition and genuine entrepreneurship in the bus industry. One stated, after his anonymity had been guaranteed (several of his former employees later worked for Crosville in management positions), that 'They had a fully loaded cheque-book issued by the proverbial Bank of Hell and they were determined to use it to eliminate every last bit of competition. You tell me, who is the 'pirate'? Is it the man who returns from the war, establishes a small family business, charges the lowest fares he can, and is proud to be of service to his community? Or is it the wealthy man who comes here from another country, colonising us like the bloody Normans, and offering to drive us out of business if we don't accept his money?'

I assured the octogenarian veteran in question that my own allegiances were to the independent camp. He pointed to WJ Crosland-Taylor's books on a shelf in the corner. 'It's about time that somebody told our side of the story.' As I was leaving his home after a very enjoyable afternoon his eyes twinkled as he said 'Tell you what though. Crosville has gone and many of us are still here. We've outlasted them all, the father, the sons, and the company.'

Author's Note

As with the two earlier volumes in my series on independent bus operators, limitations of space have imposed a time limit for inclusion in this book. On this occasion only those operators involved in stage carriage operations (excluding restricted works and schools services) in 1953 or later have been allowed an individual entry, arranged alphabetically within each geographical area defined by the chapter headings. Important pre-1939 operators have already been (briefly) dealt with in this Introduction, and those which

survived into the period between 1945 and 1952 are also mentioned in passing in the text. The only wilful exclusions are the small number of 'new' operators which emerged in the early 1970s, usually to replace market-day only facilities abandoned by Crosville or to operate (with subsidy) on tourist-oriented services invented by the post-1974 county councils. Most of these deliberately excluded operations were comparatively short-lived and many were operated with minibuses rather than more traditional vehicles.

At the more recent end of the chronological spectrum the 'independent era' is deemed to have ended in 1986, at the point of deregulation, after which all bus companies were (technically) independent with the exception of a small number of municipal operations which remained in the hands of local government. The ongoing stories of former 'independents' which survived the subsequent free-for-all are outlined at the end of their individual sections, but this later period is a different age and I willingly leave its history unexcavated, to be found by younger hands than mine. I would suggest that 2036 might be a good time to start looking at the post-deregulation era in depth – by then it should be possible to place it all in perspective!

Neville Mercer
November 2011

ACKNOWLEDGMENTS

Any serious historian attempting to record the histories of Britain's independent bus operators must combine three separate elements to produce a coherent whole; the vehicles used, the routes operated, and the personalities involved. With regard to the vehicles, this present book was considerably harder to write than its two predecessors (covering Staffordshire and Shropshire), as no published sources existed to provide details of pre-1970 fleet histories.

This obstacle was partly overcome by long hours spent in the archive of the Greater Manchester Transport Society, studying back issues of PSV Circle news-sheets for the period from 1957 to 1969. My sincerest thanks are extended to the Manchester Museum of Transport's archivist, George Turnbull, for his enthusiastic assistance during my many visits. Another of the museum's activists, David Thomas, also made a significant

Western Transport was formed by combining the BET dominated Wrexham & District operation with the far-flung North Wales interests of the Great Western Railway. The company existed for less than three years before being merged into Crosville, so comparatively few vehicles were delivered new to Western Transport. This is UN 4488, one of a batch of 16 Tilling-Stevens B10A2s with 32-seat Brush bodywork delivered to Western in 1931. It passed to Crosville in 1933 but was sold off rather prematurely along with the rest of the batch in 1938. *(Author's Collection)*

This, believe it or not, is the digitally enhanced version of this photograph – you should see the original! It is included for its rarity value. The vehicle is UC 1816, one of a pair of Maudslay ML3 buses acquired by Rothwell of Holt (near Wrexham) in 1928, The 30-seat bodywork is by Hall Lewis, a company which later changed its name to Park Royal. The Rothwell business passed to Crosville in 1933 and the ML3s served briefly with that operator (UC 1816 as fleet number 978) but were sold in 1934. *(C Carter via Peter Harden)*

Hughes of Llansilin's first real motor-bus was this Ford Model T, CA 2151. Built in 1915 as a lorry, it had received this 7-seat 'Dixi' body before acquisition by Hughes in 1926. The founder of the business, EP Hughes, is on the left and one of his three sons to the right. *(Malcolm Knight Collection)*

EP Hughes' second PSV was this unidentified char-a-banc, seen outside the Jones Bros farm supplies shop in Llansilin. The vehicle is named 'Lily of the Valley' and its registration plate ends with the numbers '6052' or (possibly) '8052'. Lancia and Straker have both been suggested as the manufacturer of the chassis. *(John Carroll via Malcolm Knight)*

contribution to this book by giving me access to both his personal memories of some of the operators and his command of the Welsh language.

As some readers will be aware, the PSV Circle's news-sheets only extended their coverage to small operators in 'the provinces' in 1957, so details of earlier vehicles had to be found elsewhere in that organisation's impressive records. Access to this pre-1957 material was provided by John Kaye, and I cannot thank John enough for the generous contribution of his time, knowledge, and moral support during the preparation of this book. The material he made available to me included photocopies of the handwritten notes of the PSV Circle's local editors and 'roving reporters' and extracts from the official motor taxation records for the area, and without his help the fleet histories of many North Wales operators would have remained skeletal at best.

Most of the information concerning the stage carriage services of the North Wales independents was painfully prised from the 'Notices & Proceedings' of the North West Traffic Commissioners, but the set of this publication on file at the Manchester Museum of Transport has some significant gaps, making other sources a necessity. My thanks go to Dave Cunningham for stepping into the breach and providing me with information from both his own research and from the (as yet unpublished) notes of Ken Swallow. Dave is a former Crosville manager and I hope that he will forgive me for my unkind words about the Taylor family!

I first came up with the idea of a book on North Wales independents in 1988, and conducted a series of interviews with proprietors between then and 1992 when I was forced to shelve the project because of family and work commitments. Much of the information about 'personalities' collected back then has been incorporated into the present volume. In the modern recessionary era fewer proprietors have proven willing to contribute their perspectives (time becomes more valuable as profit margins shrink), but notable exceptions have been provided by Dafydd Jones of the Clynnog & Trefor Motor Co and Eric W Jones of Express Motors. Their assistance in this endeavour is noted with thanks.

Several other individuals have also helped to provide information, including Lawrence Corrieri, Mike Grant, Peter Jenner, Berwyn Prys Jones, John Owen, Keith Phillips, Ian Read, and Peter Tulloch, and my gratitude is extended to one and all.

PHOTOGRAPHIC CREDITS

Venture's 'Super Prestige' series is rightly renowned for its photographic coverage, a tradition continued with this book. Individual images are credited to their source in the accompanying captions whenever possible, but and to all I am very grateful. However, special mention must be made of the contributions by Roy Marshall (surely one of the finest bus photographers of all time), Alan Oxley of the Omnibus Society (who provided prints from several rare Roy Marshall negatives), and three gentlemen who opened their entire collections to me and between them provided more than a third of the photographs in this book. These stalwarts of my 'photographic support network' are Nick Craig, Peter Harden, and the well-known transport historian DJ Stanier. Large numbers of black and white prints were also provided by Tony Beasley, postcard collector Margaret Jones, Ray Jones (no relation), Malcolm Knight and TG Turner, while the colour coverage was made more comprehensive by contributions from the lenses and/or collections of Martyn Hearson, Geoff Lumb, Vic Nutton, and JT Williams.

Some of the images which arrived on my doormat were of less than ideal quality and have been enhanced by the computer magic of my enormously talented daughter, Helena Mercer. Those who wish to carp about their current presentability should take a look at the originals – she really has worked wonders to help me portray some rare and eccentric vehicles.

At this point I offer my sincere apologies to anyone who has been omitted from this 'roll of honour'. Such an omission is purely accidental – my filing system is slightly chaotic – and no insult is intended. In closing my thanks go to John Senior, Mark Senior, Bob Rowe and Ian Stubbs of Venture Publications for their faith, guidance, and encouragement during the preparation of this book. We collectively hope that you enjoy our efforts.

PART ONE

CAERNARVONSHIRE & ANGLESEY

The traditional county of Caernarvonshire was bounded by the Menai Strait and the Irish Sea to the north and west, Cardigan Bay and Merionethshire to the south, and Denbighshire to the east. Most of the eastern boundary was delineated by the River Conway, but at the estuary of this river the county included an enclave on the east bank around the rocky headland known as the Great Orme. Caernarvonshire's largest town during the period covered by this book was Llandudno, in the shadow of the Great Orme, which had expanded from a small village with around 1,000 inhabitants in 1847 into a bustling seaside resort with more than 20,000 permanent residents by the middle of the 20th century. The next largest community was Bangor, the only cathedral city in North Wales, which grew thanks to the arrival of the railway in the second half of the 19th century and the establishment of a university in the first half of the 20th to a population of 13,000 plus almost as many students. Caernarvon itself, the county town, had around 10,000 people, and other important communities included Conway and the Cardigan Bay resort of Pwllheli, the largest town on the Lleyn peninsula with almost 4,000 residents.

Across the Menai Strait, which was only 300 yards wide at its narrowest point, lay the county of Anglesey, consisting of the island of Anglesey (the largest in the Irish Sea) and several much smaller islands. The largest of these was Holy Island to the northwest, joined to its superior neighbour by bridges for both road and railway. Holyhead, a port since prehistoric times, was the county of Anglesey's most important town with more than 11,000 inhabitants, boosted by the seaport and later additions such as a major aluminium smelter and the major RAF base at Valley a few miles away on the main island. On Anglesey itself the largest community was Llangefni in the centre of the island (a market town with more than 4,000 residents), followed by Amlwch in the northeast and the adjacent communities of Beaumaris and Menai Bridge in the southeast.

Caelloi Motors of Pwllheli

In 1851 a young farmworker, Thomas Hughes, had an accident which left him incapable of further heavy labour. The Victorian era was unsympathetic to such misfortune and he faced catastrophe. Luckily for him the people of his home community, the village of Dinas in the central highlands of the Lleyn peninsula, were less callous than the British ruling-class of the time. A local farmer gave him a horse, another contributed a pair of cart wheels, and Hughes built a makeshift body to create a conveyance suitable for both passengers and goods. He then became a 'village carrier', operating on-demand trips to nearby towns including Pwllheli on the south coast of the peninsula and Nevin to the north.

Hughes' daughter married Thomas Jones, who became involved in his father-in-law's business, and in 1869 the family benefited greatly from the arrival of the railway age in Pwllheli. The small town, then little more than a fishing village, prospered in the subsequent decades and by the turn of the century had become a tourist resort with its own bijou tramway. As the pace of technological change continued to accelerate, the injured farmworker's grandson, Thomas Hughes Jones, realised that the time of horse-drawn transportation would soon be coming to an end and began to consider the purchase of a motor vehicle.

The First World War delayed the conversion to petrol power, but in January 1923 the family acquired a Traffic lorry (registered CC 3175) which could be converted to carry 20 passengers as well as freight. A year later Thomas Hughes Jones became the sole proprietor of the business and adopted the title of Caelloi Motors, named after a 30 acre farmstead near Dinas which had become his family's home.

Caelloi's next known vehicle was a new 14-seat Morris (CC 7722) which arrived in November 1927, followed by a similarly sized REO in November 1931. The latter machine (JC 346) lasted for 18 years, although the last six of these were spent as a lorry. From 1943 its passenger duties were usurped by a trio of Bedfords, composed of second-hand examples of the 20-seat WLB and 26-seat WTB and a 32-seat OWB utility bus. The OWB operated most of the journeys on Caelloi's two stage carriage routes, licensed in 1931, from the Dinas area direct to

CWB 982 was originally a double-decker supplied to Sheffield Corporation in 1936. After the war the Leyland TD4c Titan was acquired by a dealer who scrapped its first body and replaced it with a 33-seat coach unit by Burlingham. Caelloi Motors of Pwllheli bought it in June 1958 and kept it in service until February 1961. *(Roy Marshall via the Omnibus Society)*

Sentinel STC4/40 bus JWF 176 was new to Connor & Graham of Easington in March 1951 and spent more than nine years on their stage services to the east of Hull. In September 1960 it travelled across the entire breadth of Great Britain to reach its second operator, Caelloi of Pwllheli. The 40-seat machine was to prove rather underpowered for the Lleyn peninsula, but lasted until November 1964 before being sold off to an operator in flatter terrain. *(Roy Marshall)*

This Tiger Cub with 41-seat coach bodywork by Alexander started life as a Leyland Motors demonstrator, hence the Lancashire registration TTB 80. Caelloi bought it from Harris of Glasgow in June 1961 and used it alongside the Sentinel on the stage services from Pwllheli to Dinas. While the STC4/40 retained its basic Connor & Graham colour scheme (red and cream), the Tiger Cub was painted into Caelloi's new livery of pink and white. In October 1964 it was sold to Finchley Coaches, and would later find its way to Partridge of Hadleigh. It was destroyed by fire in Partridge's yard before preservationists could save it for posterity. *(Author's Collection)*

I wonder where the registration mark is now? On a black BMW somewhere? GUN 2 was one of a pair of Foden PVSC6 coaches with fully-fronted Metalcraft bodywork delivered to Pye of Colwyn Bay in 1950. It was later transferred to Pye's associate company, Hancock of Old Colwyn, and then moved over to Pwllheli for use by Caelloi Motors – by then the parent of Pye itself. The vehicle is seen here in Pwllheli working the stage service to Dinas, a duty it shared with a Bristol LWL6B 'Queen Mary' coach after the departure of the Sentinel and the Tiger Cub. *(Phil Sposito via Tony Beasley)*

Pwllheli (on six days per week) and from Dinas to Pwllheli via Llaniestyn and Garn (on Wednesdays and Saturdays).

In the post-war years Thomas Hughes Jones' son, Thomas Herbert Jones, became increasingly active in the business and the two men made the decision to move their main base to the Pwllheli end of the route in 1946, while maintaining an out-station in Dinas. Their new premises, known as the West End Garage, had previously been the depot of Pwllheli's (by then defunct) horse-drawn tramway service. The economic impetus for this expansion had been provided by the establishment of a Butlin's holiday camp in Pwllheli, resulting in a large increase in demand for coaching capacity. The Caelloi fleet grew apace with this demand. A pre-war Leyland SKP Cub arrived in 1947 and was joined by several other pre-war coaches over the next five years.

Among the purchases during this period the most significant was CXL 651, a 1936 AEC Regal with Harrington bodywork, acquired from the George Ewer (Grey Green) group of London in May 1948. The Jones family were impressed by this machine and most future coaches would be of 'heavyweight' construction, although the majority would be of Leyland manufacture. Three pre-war TS7/TS8 Tigers were acquired in 1950-2, and were followed by two (even older) TD2 Titans which had originally served Oldham and Salford Corporations as double-decker buses but had been rebodied by a dealer as coaches after the war.

The company's first post-war vehicles, a pair of Bedford OBs first registered to Yorkshire operators, finally arrived in January 1955. One was a Mulliner-bodied bus which became the principal vehicle on the stage carriage routes, the other a Duple-bodied coach which was swiftly replaced by an even more modern Bedford SBO/Duple Super Vega acquired from Greatrex of Stafford. This vehicle, 924 BRE, was acquired to fulfil Thomas Herbert Jones' dream of operating extended coach tours as another source of revenue. Less expensive (and considerably older) coaches also continued to arrive, including another pre-war Regal in March 1957 and a further rebodied Titan – this one a TD4c originally operated by Sheffield Corporation – in June 1958. Between these two veterans (in February 1958) the company bought its first underfloor-engined vehicle, a 1952 AEC Regal IV with Burlingham Seagull bodywork

which replaced the SBO on the extended tours programme.

A second Regal IV, but on this occasion with avant-garde Windover Kingsway bodywork, arrived from Sheffield United Tours in November 1959. By coincidence another Windover-bodied machine arrived in the same month, although this was a fully-fronted PS1 Tiger which came from Hebble and mainly found work on the stage carriage services despite its coach seating. Pwllheli was a long way from almost everywhere, but the intriguing mixture of vehicles to be found in the Caelloi fleet began to attract enthusiasts to a Butlin's holiday in large numbers.

The following decade began with an even more unusual vehicle, a 40-seat Sentinel STC4/40 which had previously served with Connor & Graham in the East Riding of Yorkshire and replaced the Mulliner-bodied OB as the rostered vehicle on the direct route from Dinas. A second-hand Duple-bodied AEC Reliance coach purchased in March 1961 proved to be of more lasting significance, as the vast majority of all future coach acquisitions would be Reliance variants until the model became unobtainable. One exception was an Alexander-bodied Tiger Cub, a former Leyland demonstrator, which came hot on the heels of the first Reliance in June 1961. This vehicle joined the Sentinel as a regular on the stage carriage services until 1964 when both were sold.

In what some observers perceived as a retrograde step the underfloor-engined Sentinel and Tiger Cub were replaced by older machines with their engines at the front. These included two Regal IIIs with fully-fronted Duple bodywork and a similarly styled Bristol LWL6B with ECW 'Queen Mary' bodywork acquired from Bristol Omnibus in August 1965. Although older than the vehicles they replaced they had the advantage of more luxurious seating, and as all stage services were operated by a driver and conductor the lack of a front entrance was largely irrelevant. They could also be used, in an emergency, to operate 'local' excursions which made them superior to the bus seated Sentinel or the under-powered Tiger Cub.

Caelloi's first 36ft long coach also arrived in 1965, a two year old Bedford VAL14 with Duple Vega Major bodywork acquired from an operator in Preston. It was mainly used on 'local' excursion work where its 52-seat capacity saved many a duplicate carrying a partial load to avoid turning people away. Meanwhile, the extended tours programme had been producing good returns, and the Jones family decided to expand its activities in this respect to catchment areas beyond the bounds of Caernarvonshire. In the summer of 1965 the family acquired a controlling shareholding in the long-established coaching firm of Pye of Colwyn Bay, including its subsidiary company Hancock of Old Colwyn. Caelloi's potential market for its tours more than doubled as a result, enabling the Jones' to offer a far more varied selection of dates and destinations.

There were also some interesting vehicle transfers between the Pwllheli and Colwyn Bay operations. Notable among these was the arrival at the West End Garage of a Foden PVSC6 coach, new to Pye and later with Hancock, which was used on the stage carriage routes alongside the ex-Bristol Omnibus 'Queen Mary'. Sadly, the days of both machines were numbered as car ownership increased and revenues from the Dinas services fell. In 1968 it was decided that conductors would have to go, and two Tiger Cub buses suitable for driver-only operation (one with Saunders-Roe bodywork built at Beaumaris, the other with a Weymann body) were acquired from Northern General. They looked quite fetching in Caelloi's new pink and white livery (which had replaced the company's previous red and cream colour scheme) and the Weymann-bodied example was further enhanced by the addition of as rectangular radiator grille. As far as can be ascertained this was a purely decorative feature.

Another major change took place in 1970 when the Colwyn Bay operation was sold to a locally based consortium which included members of the Pye family, having proven too difficult to administer properly from distant Pwllheli. Caelloi kept the extended tours part of the business and bought two 36ft long Reliances to expand the European part of its programme. These vehicles, new to Global Tours of London, had stylish Duple (Northern) Continental bodywork with 44 luxurious seats in place of the more usual 51. One of the pair was sold to Clynnog & Trevor (qv) in 1973, but the other remained with Caelloi for more than a decade.

Thomas Hughes Jones passed away in the early 1970s after 50 years of service to the company and his place in the Caelloi partnership was taken by his grandson Eryl Jones. Other developments in the 1970s included some interesting vehicle purchases. By 1975 good second-hand Reliance coaches were becoming difficult to find and Caelloi acquired its first Volvo B58 coach. Many more would follow. In the same year the partnership acquired its first ever double-deckers, two Bristol FS6B Lodekkas which came from Red & White to operate schools contracts. The Lodekkas were followed in 1976 by a Barton BTS2/Plaxton coach acquired from a firm in Bradford. This was basically a rebuilt, lengthened, and rebodied AEC Reliance, in this case a machine which Barton had bought from the Creamline group in Hampshire. Several other North Wales operators acquired BTS2s, so the purchase seemed less odd than it might have appeared elsewhere.

At the end of 1976 the stage carriage routes received a fresh investment in the shape of two Park Royal-bodied AEC Reliance dual-purpose vehicles. They were acquired from West Riding but had been new to Hebble, and replaced a Bedford C5Z1/Duple (Midland) 30-seater which had taken over from the two Northern General Tiger Cubs but had proven to be unequal to the task. The Reliances were painted in Caelloi's new black and white livery; most of us would have preferred to see them in shocking pink.

In 1977 the Lodekkas used on schools work were sold (one of them, AAX 23B, went to the USA and might still exist) and were replaced by two Atlanteans with Weymann lowbridge bodywork which had been new to East Midland and Maidstone & District. Both Atlanteans were immediately fitted with (entirely non-functional) Lodekka radiator grilles and looked extremely odd. They too were repainted in the black and white livery which had become standard for the coaching fleet several years previously.

The stage services continued to decline and by 1978 had been combined with schools journeys although still available to the general public. In 1986, with deregulation imminent, it was decided to cease commercial operation of the Dinas routes which then passed to Nefyn Coaches under a Gwynedd County Council contract. It was a case of swings and roundabouts. Although the original stage services had gone, Caelloi was the successful bidder to operate several other tendered services including an important route from Pwllheli to Portmadoc (or Porthmadog as it had become by that time).

From 1961 onwards Caelloi turned to second-hand AEC Reliances for its coaching operations. CEW 45C was a 2MU4RA version with a 43-seat Plaxton Panorama body. New to Whippet of Hilton in 1965, it came to Caelloi in June 1969 and is seen close to Caelloi's West End Garage in the pink and white livery. The similar vehicle to the rear is in the later black and pale cream colour scheme. *(John Kaye)*

Caelloi's first double-deckers were a pair of rear entrance Lodekkas acquired from Red & White. The Lodekkas were sold in 1977 and replaced by two 'lowbridge' Atlanteans, one from the East Midland fleet and the other from Maidstone & District. Both were fitted with entirely cosmetic Lodekka radiator grilles which made them look very odd indeed. This is the former M&D example, 53 DKT, retired in May 1980 and seen here in a dealer's yard after disposal, still in Caelloi's black and cream livery. *(JT Williams Collection)*

A mixture of new traffic brought in by the Butlin's holiday camp at Pwllheli and the general surge in travel after the Second World War made double-deckers a necessity for the Clynnog & Trevor Motor Co. The first examples were pre-war machines on their last legs, but C&T soon invested in some brand-new specimens including two Guy Arab IIIs with Meadows 6DC engines and 56-seat Barnard bodywork. This one, seen in Castle Square in Caernarvon, is JC 9790 and was delivered in March 1949. It was withdrawn from use in June 1962. *(Clynnog & Trevor Motor Co)*

The company's third new double-decker was a Crossley DD42 with Crossley 56-seat bodywork which had briefly served as a demonstrator, hence its Stockport registration. DJA 434, first registered in October 1949, came to Clynnog & Trevor in January 1950 and lasted until May 1965. *(Clynnog & Trevor Motor Co)*

The two Atlanteans had gone in 1980 after the loss of the schools contracts and the next double-decker to arrive was a former Greater Manchester 'Standard', acquired shortly after deregulation for a special service to Butlin's restyled 'Suncoast World'. It was followed in 1990 by a pair of Bristol VRT3/ECW double-deckers which were used on the service to Porthmadog and other Gwynedd contracts until they were sold to Alpine of Llandudno in 1995.

By the time this book is published Caelloi Motors will be in its 90th year as a motor-bus operator and its 161st year as a provider of public transport. Remarkably, the company is still managed by a direct descendant of the founder and is still a private partnership rather than a limited company. It is also one of the major operators of extended coach tours aimed at the Welsh market and its smartly turned out coaches can be seen all over the British Isles and in many parts of the European mainland. Thomas Hughes would be very proud of his descendants and might consider that his farmyard accident so long ago had been a stroke of luck in disguise.

Clynnog & Trevor Motor Co

The first motor-buses in North Wales were introduced by railway operators, by the GWR in the east and by the Cambrian Railways group in the west. Early examples of the species, such as the pair of Orions used by the Cambrian on their feeder service from the Nevin area to Pwllheli, proved to be fairly unreliable, but the technology was advancing rapidly and it soon became obvious that the age of the horse-drawn village carrier's cart was about to end. Express Motors began a regular service from its base at Rhostryfan to Caernarvon in 1909, and in 1912 three motor-buses were delivered to three operators on the Lleyn peninsula. Tocia, Nevin Green, and the Abersoch company were unanimous in their choice of Karriers (made in Huddersfield like George Crosland Taylor), but the next operator to emerge in the area opted for a vehicle manufactured by Commer in London.

The newcomer, registered as the Clynnog & Trevor Motor Company Ltd on 1st April 1912, was unusual in another way. While most independent operations were overseen by their individual proprietors and founders, Clynnog & Trevor

came into existence as a publicly owned company with a wide range of shareholders from the two villages in its title. The founding fathers included AWS Williams Esq of Clynnog (described as a 'gentleman') and William Williams of Trevor (a labourer) along with three local farmers, two sett-makers, a joiner, and a church minister. Their signatures to the company's articles of association were witnessed by Richard R Jones, the village schoolteacher in Clynnog, who became the company secretary.

The 35-seat Commer arrived at Trevor in July 1912 and was put to work on an ambitious service from Caernarvon to Pwllheli. At an early stage the company received the local nickname 'Moto Coch' (Red Motors) in reference to its chosen livery. Generations of English visitors have presumed that this actually meant Motor Coach in Welsh.

The stage carriage route was an instant success and a second Commer arrived in July 1913 to enable the frequency to be increased. Further expansion was postponed by the First World War, with a third Commer eventually arriving in August 1920. It would be the last of its type with C&T for many years as the next vehicle was a 32-seat Karrier delivered in February 1922. The new machine replaced the 1912 Commer. A second Karrier came from a rival operator, Owen of Trevor, in April 1924 and a third of the type was delivered from the Huddersfield factory in July 1925. The last of C&T's four Karriers, a 26-seat CL4 (also brand-new), arrived in June 1926. By then the company's fleet had grown to five vehicles as the last of the Commers survived until 1929.

After a brief period of Karrier ascendancy Leyland became the new manufacturer of choice. In 1928 a quartet of (bonneted) Lioness vehicles (CC 7851-4) arrived from the Lancashire firm, to be followed by a second-hand 1924 Leyland acquired from a Staffordshire company in 1929. In the same year the final Commer was replaced by a fourth-hand Thornycroft X with an interesting history. This 24-seater (EC 3510) had been new to the Lake District Road Traffic Co in 1920, had passed with that business into the ownership of Lancashire & Westmorland Motor Services, and then by the same means to Ribble in December 1927. It gave a further two years of service to C&T before being replaced by yet another Leyland, a PLSC3 Lion (TE 713) which had been new to Freeman (Silver Star) of Chorley but also came to C&T via Ribble.

The company's decision to start services to several villages situated on narrow country lanes, such as Pencaenewydd, required something smaller and more manoeuvrable and this led to the acquisition of a 14-seat GMC in June 1930. It was soon replaced by a 20-seat Guy which more accurately reflected the level of passenger demand for the services.

After all of this frantic expansion a quieter period ensued and for around five years no further vehicles were acquired. The next three were all Leylands, a third-hand TS1 Tiger in 1935, and new examples of the KPZ2 Cub (in 1936) and LT5 Lion (in 1937). With Adolf Hitler seizing territory from surrounding nations and an outbreak of war generally agreed to be inevitable, it was perhaps surprising that the next two deliveries (in October 1938 and January 1939) were German built Opel Blitz 26-seaters. They apparently came with a generous supply of spare parts as both remained in service until January 1952. The company's first Bedford, a 26-seat WTB, arrived in July 1939 (presumably due to the fact that Opels had become unavailable as the factory where they were made was turned over to Panzer tank production) and it was followed by three OWB utility buses in 1943-4 (by which time the Opel factory had been destroyed by RAF bombers).

Deliveries in the immediate post-war period were far more interesting than the drab OWBs and included the company's first double-deckers, two Leyland TD1 Titans acquired from the corporations of Leicester and Warrington in the autumn of 1946. Warrington provided another pre-war Titan, on this occasion a TD2 variant, in May 1947. Single-deck acquisitions in the same period included a 1932 Daimler, a 1935 SKP3 Cub, and a brand-new Bedford OB/Mulliner bus delivered in January 1948.

The pre-war Titans had been invaluable in helping the company to cope with the peacetime boom in traffic, but by the end of the decade were well past their prime. Their three replacements were equally fascinating; two brand-new Guy Arab IIIs with Barnard bodywork (which arrived in November 1948 and March 1949), and an all-Crossley DD42/7 which replaced the TD2 in January 1950. The Crossley had briefly served as a demonstrator and thus carried a Stockport registration despite being, to all intents and purposes, a factory fresh vehicle. One presumes that a healthy discount was offered by Crossley as a third Arab III would have been the more obvious choice.

Second-hand acquisitions during 1949 were an ex-Ribble TS6 Tiger (CK 4732 which had been more recently operated by Corvedale in Shropshire) and an ex-Yorkshire Woollen District LT5 Lion (HD 4601) which arrived in July after a side trip to Blackpool to be rebodied as a 33-seat coach by HV Burlingham. The TS6 had gone before the end of 1955 but the updated LT5 lasted until July 1962 and was one of the last of its type in revenue earning service. There were also some interesting single-deckers in the 1950s intake, including a pair of 35-seat Roe-bodied Albion CX11 buses from Hebble (both were retired in 1953) and a Leyland TS7 Tiger from East Midland. The latter, formerly a bus registered BRR 929, was sent to Metalcraft to be rebodied as a coach before entering service with the new Caernarvonshire registration ACC 695. It was an attractive mongrel and was eventually withdrawn in August 1964.

From 1951 until 1959 the majority of purchases were of pre-war origin, possibly a reflection of the fact that C&T was still making hefty repayments on its new double-deckers of 1949/50 at a time when traffic had already started to decline. Double-deck acquisitions during the decade were all TD series Titans including examples from Hants & Dorset, Southern Vectis, PMT, and Ribble. The Hants & Dorset example was a TD1 (TK 3884) and its original Leyland lowbridge body had been so extensively 'refurbished' by Portsmouth Aviation that it was barely recognisable as a 1930 vehicle, while the Southern Vectis example was TF 6821 – already referred to in the Introduction to this book. This machine had started life in 1931 as a TD1 demonstrator with Leyland highbridge bodywork and was then sold to Cardiff Corporation. Cardiff passed it on to Southern Vectis in 1945. Four years later the Isle of Wight operator attempted to make it more 'Tilling friendly' by fitting it with a new ECW lowbridge body and a Gardner 5LW engine. It came to C&T in 1954 and the Gardner engine was immediately removed and replaced with a more appropriate Leyland E181 unit. In this configuration the machine survived until 1961.

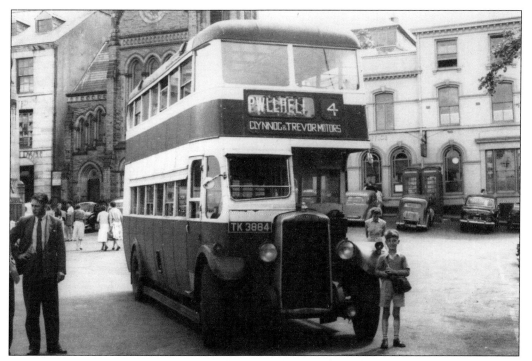

TK 3884 was a Leyland TD1 Titan, originally delivered to Hants & Dorset in 1931 with standard Leyland lowbridge bodywork. By the end of the Second World War the vehicle was worse for wear and was sent to Portsmouth Aviation for refurbishment. As can be seen, they modified its bodywork extensively. Clynnog & Trevor bought the machine in December 1951 and kept it until October 1955. *(RHG Simpson via TG Turner)*

And here is another 1931 vintage TD1 with an interesting history. TF 6821 was built as a demonstrator for Leyland Motors and originally carried a Leyland highbridge body. Sold off after a year to Cardiff Corporation, it spent 13 years in the Welsh city before being sold to Southern Vectis in 1945 as their fleet number 708. Four years later they decided to 'Tillingise' it and fitted it with an ECW lowbridge body and a Gardner 5LW engine. Clynnog & Trevor bought it in 1954 and immediately replaced the Gardner engine with a more appropriate Leyland E181 unit. It gave seven years of service in this, its final, form. *(Nick Craig Collection)*

Clynnog & Trevor's single decker fleet was also a fascinating mix of vehicles. AEC Regal III coach KWA 708 had 33-seat Windover Huntingdon bodywork and came to C&T from Sheffield United Tours in June 1957. Seen here at Caernarvon Quay in July 1966, it was withdrawn from use two months later. *(Nick Craig)*

Ribble was by far the largest customer for the 44-seat Sentinel STC6/44 bus, taking 14 of them in 1951. Despite their non-standard nature in a fleet dominated by Leylands they enjoyed a full life with Ribble and were retired in 1963. DRN 348 was acquired by C&T in September 1963 but according to most reports was only used in service by them for a matter of weeks, despite being licensed until June 1964. It retained its basic Ribble livery. Here it is parked alongside the garage at Trevor, cheekily showing 'N82' in its route blind box – this was Crosville's number for the Caernarvon-Pwllheli service and C&T vehicles with number blinds usually showed '082'. *(Clynnog & Trevor Motor Co)*

GFM 891 was a Bristol K6A with a 55-seat lowbridge ECW body, new to Crosville in 1947 as their fleet number MB283. Later renumbered as DKA283 it came to C&T (via a dealer) in April 1962, one of a pair acquired to replace the (younger) Arab III double-deckers of 1948/9. *(John Fozard via DJ Stanier)*

The two K6As and the Crossley were replaced by a pair of Regent IIIs acquired from City of Oxford Motor Services. SFC 435 (formerly COMS fleet number L169) had lowbridge bodywork by Park Royal and came to C&T in October 1965. The vehicle survived into the 1970s and was destined to be C&T's last double-decker for almost a decade before the arrival of an ex-London DMS Fleetline. *(Peter Yeomans via Tony Beasley)*

Way back in 1912 Clynnog & Trevor's first vehicle had been a Commer, and the marque returned to the fleet in 1964 when two Commer-Beadle T48 coaches were bought from Birch Bros of London. PYK 62, formerly Birch's fleet number K62, was a 41-seater and is seen in Caernarvon in January 1967. In August of that year it was replaced by a similar machine seen below. *(Nick Craig)*

C&T's next Commer-Beadle T48s had 41-seat bus bodywork and came from Devon General. TTT 792 (formerly DG's fleet number SC792) arrived in July 1967, and is seen in Caernarvon in March 1968 displaying 'Pwllheli 082' on its blinds. *(Nick Craig)*

Leyland single-deckers of pre-war provenance included Tigers from North Western (two), Ribble (one), and Wilts & Dorset (two). The Wilts & Dorset machines were 1930 vintage TS1s but survived with C&T until 1956. All but one of the post-war vehicles acquired during the 1950s were coaches; a two year old OB/Duple Vista which arrived in 1951, a Crossley SD42 with Trans-United bodywork which had been new to a Cheshire operator but came from Salopia of Whitchurch, and three AEC Regal IIIs which had started life with Sheffield United Tours. The exception was a fourth-hand Guy Arab III single-decker bus which arrived from East Midland in 1958.

The new decade started with two wartime Guy Arab double-deckers (a 'slightly' refurbished example from East Midland and a PMT machine which had received a new Northern Counties body with platform doors), an AEC Regent/Willowbrook double-decker from Trent, and a TS7 coach which had been fitted with fully-fronted Burlingham Sunsaloon bodywork after the war by its previous owner, Creams of Llandudno. The only acquisition in 1961 was a Bedford SB/Plaxton coach from Yorkshire Traction but 1962 brought another Regent/Willowbrook double-decker from Trent, a Regal/Willowbrook saloon from the same source (RC 9699, which had been 'modernised' with a full-front in 1958) and a Bristol K6A/ECW double-decker from Crosville via a neutral dealership. The second Regent and the K6A replaced the two Arab III/Barnard double-deckers which were suffering from deteriorating bodywork. Another K6A/ECW was smuggled in from Crosville in June 1963 and replaced the rebodied Arab/Northern Counties double-decker from PMT.

The single-deck part of the fleet had lost most of its pre-war vehicles by the end of 1964, but their replacements were equally fascinating. A Sentinel STC6/44 arrived from Ribble but according to several witnesses was only in service for three weeks before being parked up to rot into oblivion. Commers returned to the fleet for the first time in 35 years when two T48/Beadle integral coaches (PYK 62/4) were acquired from Birch Brothers of London. Sister ships PYK 63/5 went from Birch to another North Wales company, Phillips of Bagillt in Flintshire, for use on works services. The C&T duo were used almost exclusively on the stage carriage routes and replaced the OB/Mulliner bus of 1948 and the older of the two Regent/Willowbrook double-deckers.

The other Regent/Willowbrook and the all-Crossley double-decker were retired in 1965 and their places were taken by two AEC Regent IIIs acquired from City of Oxford Motor Services. As passenger numbers fell still further the double-deck fleet was reduced and the two ex-Crosville K6As were replaced by four more Commer-Beadle T48s in 1966-8. The quartet (a 1958 coach and three 1956 buses) came from Devon General and also replaced the earlier examples of their marque which had been acquired from Birch Brothers.

By 1970 the only double-deckers left in the fleet were the two Regent IIIs and most of the stage services were being operated by the T48s and a Weymann-bodied AEC Reliance bus which had been acquired from Maidstone & District. The latter machine proved to be popular with C&T's management and three more ex-M&D Reliances were acquired in 1970/1, two with Beadle bodywork and one with a Harrington body. They replaced the Devon General T48s. The final double-decker was retired in 1974, replaced by a 36ft long AEC Reliance service bus with the same seating capacity. By a neat coincidence this also came from City of Oxford.

The C&T fleet was to remain entirely single-deck in nature for the best part of a decade although its total seating capacity actually rose in 1977 when two 36ft Reliance/Willowbrook service buses acquired from East Midland replaced two shorter Reliance buses. In 1980 they were joined by a 36ft Leyland Leopard/Weymann saloon from Ribble which allowed the final ex-M&D Reliance to be withdrawn. The next single-decker bus was more of a surprise, a Bedford YRT with Alexander Y type bodywork which was acquired from Lothian in September 1982.

Double-deckers returned to the Clynnog & Trefor fleet (the title of the company had belatedly been changed to match the revised spelling of the name of its home village) in October 1982 when a former London Transport DMS class Fleetline arrived from CK of Cardiff. It was one of the B20 versions with the peculiar diagonal shrouds above the engine bustle. A 'normal' DMS followed in June 1986. Another Fleetline came from Chester in the late 1980s but most C&T double-deckers of the newly deregulated era were Bristol VRT3s with ECW bodywork. The last of them was eventually retired in 2008.

The traditional mainline route from Caernarvon to Pwllheli via Clynnog and Trevor has continued to the present-day, now officially known as service 12, a route number imposed on C&T by Gwynedd Council. The operator had always preferred to use the unofficial designation '082' which mimicked that of Crosville's competing N82 service. The Fleetlines and the dozen or so VRT3s which followed them as the staple equipment on the route have now been replaced by low-floor single-decker types. Schools contracts are an important component of the company's revenues (hence the large number of VRT3s once owned) along with luxury coach hire and extended tours to Europe operated on behalf of assorted travel companies including Leger of far-away Rotherham.

In April 1912 the company had just nine shareholders. By 1939 this had increased to 400, almost all of them still local people, and at the time of writing there are more than 2,000. Most of these individuals are quite happy just to be involved with such a venerable North Wales institution and take no active role in the company's governance. Several are known to proudly display their share certificates in picture frames. The present management can only be congratulated for their continuing commercial success in an age when (in general) ideals seem to count for so little. Their company represents the best of the old and the best of the new.

Deiniolen Motors

The village of Deiniolen lies in the slate quarrying region of Caernarvonshire, some seven miles south from the coast and the local metropolis of Caernarvon and Bangor. Until the early 20th century the village was known as Ebenezer but changed its name to echo that of the saint memorialised in the title of the local church – or that at least was the official reason for the change. It must be suspected that the popularity of Charles Dickens' 'A Christmas Carol' and the unpopularity of that novel's principal character also had something to do with the decision.

John William Hughes (born in 1863), a younger son of an Ebenezer/Deiniolen farmer, spent most of his younger adulthood working in the huge Dinorwic slate quarry before setting himself up as an ironmonger on Deiniolen's main street. His son, William Morris Hughes, became a mechanic in the Royal Flying Corps during the First World War, and after the end of that conflict proposed to his father that they should seek a more profitable living from the motor trade. In 1919 they formed a partnership known as JW Hughes & Son and in the following year acquired a 20-seat BAT bus, bought for use on regular stage carriage services to Bangor and Caernarvon under the trading name of Rhiwen Motors. Rhiwen was the name of the family's cottage on the Rhiwlas to Deiniolen road and would also lend its name to the partnership's petrol station and car-hire business, known as Garage Rhiwen.

A 32-seat Daimler Y replaced the unreliable BAT in July 1921 and throughout the following decade the growing fleet would be composed of full-sized Daimlers and 14-seat Fords and Chevrolets. The route network also grew and by the time of the Road Traffic Act of 1930 Rhiwen Motors was operating to Caernarvon from Deiniolen and Dinorwic and to Bangor from Deiniolen (via two routes) and Llanberis. Inevitably, in January 1932, the men from Crosville arrived with cheque book and veiled threats.

The founders were reluctant to sell their thriving business, but eventually a compromise was reached. Crosville would acquire the entire operation (for the then princely sum of £24,000), except for the more rural of the two Deiniolen to Bangor services which would remain with JW Hughes & Son. The route was later extended to begin from Dinorwic. Henceforth, this remnant of the original company would trade as Deiniolen Motors, a name which had been used sporadically since 1927 alongside that of Rhiwen. Part of the money from Crosville was used to re-equip the Deiniolen fleet with more modern buses. Over the following three years a trio of Dennises arrived, a 36-seat Lancet and two 26-seat Aces, one of the latter a former Dennis demonstrator. These vehicles continued to operate the Bangor service through the Second World War and beyond.

In 1947 John William Hughes died, aged 84, and his son decided to retire. The Deiniolen business was sold to two of its employees, Thomas Henry Davies and Ivor Jones. The ageing and war-battered fleet was sold, the Lancet replaced

Long the pride of the Deiniolen Motors fleet, Crossley DD42 JC 9795 had 56-seat Crossley bodywork and was delivered in March 1949. It is seen here at the Bangor (Town Clock) terminus awaiting departure for Deiniolen and Dinorwic. In 1966 Deiniolen's sister company, Purple Motors, sold its only double-decker (an Arab III) and from then onwards the Crossley spent more time operating to Bethesda 'on hire' to Purple than with its actual legal owners. The vehicle survived until the early 1970s. *(DJ Stanier)*

Despite being widely reported as an OWB utility bus, it is believed that JC 7729 was in fact an early post-war Bedford OB with Duple's ('relaxed') Mark II service bus body. Its initial registration date of November 1946 – 18 months after the end of the war – would tend to support this belief. Deiniolen acquired it from an unknown first owner in July 1948. *(DJ Stanier)*

EUJ 635 was a Burlingham-bodied Crossley SD42 bus, new to Jones of Market Drayton in Shropshire in 1948. In May 1950 they sold it to Deiniolen Motors. Seen in Bangor, it was withdrawn from use in June 1960. *(Phil Sposito via Tony Beasley)*

Stratford Blue had a batch of Leyland PS1 Tigers with 34-seat bus bodywork by Northern Coach Builders, and after retirement by their original operator at least four of them turned up with North Wales operators. GUE 252 was acquired by Deiniolen in March 1961 and gave a further eight years of service. It is seen here at Bangor's Town Clock terminus. *(Nick Craig)*

by a newer version of the same model and the two Dennis Aces by a pair of Bedford buses, a wartime OWB and an early post-war OB. The replacement Lancet and the OWB proved to be a mere stop-gap measure as more intensive investment was to follow. The company's first (and only ever) double-decker, an all-Crossley DD42, arrived in March 1949 and replaced the OWB. An equally brand-new OB/Duple Vista coach arrived three months later, and in May 1950 the Lancet 2 was replaced by another Crossley – this time a second-hand SD42 single-decker bus with Burlingham bodywork which came from Jones of Market Drayton.

In 1952 the proprietor of a neighbouring operator, Purple Motors of Bethesda (qv) which also ran into Bangor, died with no clear successor in place to manage the business. As a result control of Purple passed to the administrator of the deceased proprietor's estate, a Mrs Pritchard, who had no wish to become involved in the bus industry at that time. After discussions with Tom Davies it was agreed that he would manage Purple Motors on her behalf, and in exchange Deiniolen's vehicles would gain access to Purple's far superior engineering facilities in Bethesda. From that point onwards the two businesses would be loyal allies although retaining their separate ownership and identities.

In June 1952 Deiniolen acquired a pre-war TS8 Tiger bus from Ribble for use on a Dinorwic quarry works service, but this vehicle would last for barely more than a year before being replaced by a post-war PS1 Tiger/Harrington coach acquired from Gliderways. The latter was not only newer but could also be used on private-hire and excursion work when not required for its Dinorwic duties. The coach remained in service until June 1959 when its position was usurped by a brand-new Bedford SB3/Duple Super Vega which assumed its leisure role but not the quarry service which was subsequently covered by a PS1 Tiger/Weymann bus acquired from PMT. The OB bus departed shortly afterwards, its 'back up' duties on the stage services devolving to the two coaches in the fleet. Another recruit arrived in December 1960 in the shape of a 1947 AEC Regal with Duple bus bodywork which replaced the single-deck Crossley. The Regal came from Thames Valley (Purple Motors received an identical machine) but had originally been owned

by Newbury & District. The ex-PMT Tiger was sold in January 1961 and its place was taken by another PS1 bus from Stratford Blue. This vehicle was part of a batch with Northern Coach Builders bodywork, almost all of which were sold to North Wales companies.

In January 1964 the Thames Valley Regal was transferred into Purple Motors ownership and replaced by another Regal acquired from a Yorkshire company. This was RKU 220 which had started life in 1948 as a half-cab coach with a Bradford company. In 1958 it had received a new (and fully-fronted) Plaxton Highway bus body and after acquisition by Deiniolen became the front-line vehicle on the Dinorwic to Bangor stage service. As a result the Crossley double-decker spent an increasing amount of its time operating 'on hire' to Purple Motors on the busier Bethesda to Bangor route. After the sale of Purple's own double-decker (a Guy Arab III) in 1966 the Crossley rarely returned to its original route but remained in Deiniolen's ownership until its withdrawal in 1972 after well over 20 years of service.

With the double-decker on more or less permanent hire to Purple, Deiniolen needed another service bus and bought an SB5 with Duple (Midland) bodywork from Williams of Ponciau in June 1966. The two vehicles allocated to the Bangor service (the SB5 and the rebodied Regal) could then both be operated by the driver alone, resulting in welcome economies, although conductors continued to be employed at times of peak demand to maintain the scheduled journey times. In May 1969 the last bus which still required a conductor by nature of its design (the Stratford Blue PS1) was retired and replaced by an underfloor-engined Tiger Cub/Saunders-Roe bus acquired from Ribble.

Ivor Jones died in the early 1970s and Tom Davies became the sole proprietor of Deiniolen Motors. In 1972 the Regal/Plaxton bus finally departed and was replaced by a Willowbrook-bodied Tiger Cub, one of a pair acquired by Mr Davies from Trent with the other going to Purple Motors. A surprise came in the following year when the SB5 bus was retired and its successor turned out to be a brand-new Bedford YRQ with 49-seat dual-purpose bodywork by Willowbrook. For the following nine years the Deiniolen bus fleet remained at three vehicles (the two Tiger

Cubs and the YRQ). The ex-Ribble Tiger Cub was eventually replaced by a 47-seat Leopard/Northern Counties bus acquired from Chester (Purple took an identical twin) but by then the writing was on the wall.

In May 1985 the stage service from Dinorwic and Deiniolen to Bangor and two vehicles were sold to Ieuan Williams (trading as Williams of Deiniolen), while the remaining bus – the Leopard – went to Purple to join its Chester sibling. Tom Davies continued to be active in the local bus industry for some time as the managing director of Purple Motors of Bethesda.

Express Motors of Rhostryfan

In 1908 Owen William Owen of Rhostryfan (a small village in the foothills of Snowdonia, to the south of Caernarvon) decided to buy a motor vehicle. Owen was employed as a train driver in the local quarry at the time, but had enough seniority to avoid working on Saturdays. The unidentified vehicle (believed to be some kind of wagonette) could thus be used for excursions and private-hire work in the evenings and on Saturdays and help to pay for its own keep. Most of his Saturday business came from shoppers bound for Caernarvon and in 1909 he formalised these excursions into a timetabled service. At an undetermined point (but prior to 1914) he began to use the trading name of 'Express Motors' for this scheduled operation, which gradually expanded into a daily (except Sunday) stage carriage service.

At first Mr Owen had a monopoly on the route, which was soon extended to start from the village of Cesarea running via Rhosgadfan, Rhostryfan, and Bontnewydd to Caernarvon. As always, success invited imitation and by 1920 Express found itself competing with Silver Star of Upper Llandwrog (qv), Dixie Bus Service, Mountaineer, and Tait Motors (all of Rhosgadfan), and Tryfan Ranger of Rhostryfan. The newcomers were also attracted to the route by the withdrawal of passenger service on the local narrow-gauge railway line in 1916.

The company's earliest vehicles have evaded identification despite extensive efforts. The first recorded machine, a 32-seat Commer (CC 2506) arrived in September 1920, and was followed by a 14-seat Ford Model T (CC 4244)

in October 1923 and a 26-seat W&G (CC 6811) in November 1926. All of these were brand-new but most subsequent deliveries, as far as is known, were acquired from other operators. These included a Leyland Lioness from Devon General, a 20-seat Guy, a 20-seat Leyland Cub, and a Commer Centaur. The latter two vehicles (GV 883 and JL 2067 respectively) were still in service at the outbreak of war in September 1939 along with a 7-seat Austin licensed as a PSV (YH 5718).

The founder's daughter, Myfanwy Owen, had married Robert Hughes Jones who was related to the proprietors of both Dixie Bus Service (his cousins) and Mountaineer (his uncle on his mother's side). At the end of the war his uncle, Owen E Hughes, decided to retire from the bus industry and sold his two surviving vehicles (both Bedford WLBs) and his stage carriage licence to his nephew. The older of the two Mountaineer WLBs was replaced by a brand-new Commer Commando with 32-seat bus bodywork by Myers & Bowman in August 1946 and it remains uncertain whether this vehicle was ordered by the old proprietor or the new one. Upon delivery it was registered to Robert Hughes Jones.

Meanwhile, his father-in-law's business, Express Motors, had come out of the war with only one serviceable vehicle, an OWB utility bus allocated to the company in 1944 to replace the increasingly decrepit Cub and Centaur. Faced with the task of rebuilding his fleet after 39 years at the helm, Mr Owen decided to retire and sold his business to his son-in-law in January 1947. The fleet under Robert Hughes Jones' direction at that point (which continued under the Express Motors name) was thus composed of a pre-war WLB, a wartime OWB, and a five month old Commer Commando. More vehicles were urgently needed to maintain the schedules and materialised in the shape of a pre-war Bedford WTB 26-seater from a Yorkshire operator, and a Leyland Cub of a similar vintage from FW Strange of Wrexham, a company recently acquired by Crosville.

Another new Commer Commando/Myers & Bowman bus arrived in June 1948, and in July a 1938 Dodge SBF with coach bodywork by Grose was acquired from the Dixie Bus Service. Dixie ceased to trade at that time, suggesting that the Jones cousins might have come to some kind of

Bedford SB5/Duple (Midland) bus 1600 UN was new to Williams of Ponciau, near Wrexham, in December 1961. In June 1966 they sold it to Deiniolen Motors. The vehicle is seen here outside Purple Motors' premises in Bethesda, presumably during a visit for maintenance purposes as no 'on hire' stickers are visible. *(Nick Craig)*

The Stratford Blue PS1's replacement was this Saunders-Roe-bodied Tiger Cub bus, FCK 844. Formerly Ribble's fleet number 412, it came to Deiniolen in May 1969 and gave them more than ten years of service before its eventual retirement. The vehicle is seen in Bangor displaying '207 Deiniolen', suggesting that it had recently operated 'on hire' to Purple Motors as '207' was that company's telephone number in Bethesda and often used as a default setting in Purple's destination displays. The Tiger Cub was saved for preservation and is currently owned (in Ribble livery) by the Anglesey Vintage Equipment Society – its bodywork was built at Beaumaris. *(Author's Collection)*

JC 9260, seen in Caernarvon, was a Commer Commando with 32-seat bus bodywork by Myers & Bowman. New to Express Motors in June 1948, it gave almost exactly nine years of service to the company before being sold for conversion into a mobile shop. *(EW Jones/Express Motors)*

In the late 1950s Express Motors began to acquire PS1 Tiger/Roe buses from a variety of major operators. The first was AHE 792 which came from Yorkshire Traction in December 1958, and is seen in this shot at Caernarvon Quay in September 1964. Williams of Llithfaen took an identical vehicle from the same batch. *(Nick Craig)*

DVH 756, another PS1/Roe, also came from Yorkshire but had been new to County Motors of Lepton. Express bought it in July 1959 and kept it for four years. It is seen in Caernarvon parked in front of a pre-war (ex-Sheffield) Leyland Titan of Whiteway. *(Tony Beasley)*

PS1 Tiger buses acquired from Lancashire United Transport rivalled those from Stratford Blue in terms of their popularity with North Wales independents, with examples to be seen in Caernarvon with Express Motors, Silver Star, and Whiteway. Express bought two of the Roe-bodied machines. It seems that JTJ 91 (acquired in March 1961) had only just arrived when this photograph was taken as it is still wearing LUT fleet number 366. *(Peter Yeomans via Nick Craig)*

Second-hand buses from operators with red liveries (such as Yorkshire Traction and LUT) were usually left in their original colour schemes after acquisition by Express Motors. The company's coaches used an entirely separate livery of green and pink in the layout illustrated here by 1305 PT, a Ford 570E Thames Trader with 41-seat Duple bodywork acquired from Gardiner of Spennymoor in May 1962. *(Nick Craig)*

By 1963 the supply of good quality second-hand PS1 buses had dried up, and in October of that year Express bought this early post-war AEC Regal/Willowbrook bus from Trent. Like the Clynnog & Trevor example illustrated on the title page, RC 9680 had started life as a 34-seat half-cab and then been rebuilt as a fully-fronted 39-seater in the late 1950s. Both machines retained their basic Trent livery while serving in the Caernarvon area which must have caused some confusion to intending passengers. *(Nick Craig)*

agreement. The Dodge was quickly replaced by a third new Commando in March 1949, although on this occasion with a coach body built by Allweather.

The first two deliveries in 1950 were both new coaches, an OB/Duple Vista in March and a PS1 Tiger/Burlingham in April. The third acquisition of the year, a 1947 OB/Mulliner bus came from Purple Motors of Bethesda (qv) in May and permitted the sale of the pre-war WTB. The fleet then stabilised until November 1953 when an increase in schools related work brought two pre-war TS8 Tiger/Burlingham buses to the Rhostryfan depot. Although new to Ribble the TS8s came from the allied Caernarvonshire fleets of Deiniolen and Purple Motors. Two further TS8s (but with coach bodies by Duple) arrived directly from Ribble in June 1954 and allowed the withdrawal of the wartime OWB utility bus which had also been demoted to schools work.

No more buses (and only one second-hand SB/Duple coach) arrived in 1955-7. By 1958/9 however the TS8s were in need of retirement and were replaced by a Beadle-bodied OB bus from Hants & Dorset and two Roe-bodied PS1 Tiger buses which came from Yorkshire Traction and County Motors of Lepton respectively. Two further PS1/Roe buses were bought from Lancashire United Transport in March 1961 and were followed by Express Motors' first AEC Regal bus, a fully-fronted Willowbrook-bodied example acquired from Trent in October 1963 to replace the former County Motors PS1. The Regal had originally been a half-cab and an identical vehicle could be seen in Caernarvon in service with Clynnog & Trevor.

Deliveries later in the decade included another PS1 bus, but on this occasion bodied by Burlingham and previously operated by Burnley, another Regal bus (with Duple bodywork) which had been built for Newbury & District but came via Thames Valley and Purple Motors, and a Bristol L6A/ECW bus bought from Crosville in 1967. The latter had been converted to forward entrance configuration while in Crosville's hands and was allegedly suited to driver only operation, although an unhealthy amount of upper body swivelling was involved in the process of fare collection.

In May 1968 Express acquired its first underfloor-engined bus, a Tiger Cub/Saunders-Roe vehicle from the Sunderland District fleet, but this was followed by three more 'traditional' buses with front engines, all from the Thames Valley fleet. The first of the three was a Bristol LL5G which had originally been delivered with a half-cab Windover coach body but had been re-equipped with a fully-fronted ECW bus body in the late 1950s to make it 'suitable' for driver only operation. It arrived in June 1968 and was followed by two more recent vintage Bristol SC4LK/ECW 35-seaters. Anyone who has ever travelled on an SC4LK knows how horrible they were, but they were cheap which made them attractive to several North Wales independents despite the noise, fumes, vibration, poor ride quality, and astonishingly poor performance on hills. The two Express Motors examples arrived in February 1970.

In October 1970 Robert Hughes Jones, having decided to concentrate on the company's coaching activities, sold the stage carriage services and three Bristol buses (the L6A, the LL5G, and one of the SC4LKs) to his neighbours and erstwhile competitors at Silver Star (qv). The Rhostryfan depot was also sold and Express moved to a new base at Bontnewydd, closer to Caernarvon. A few schools journeys were retained (along with the other SC4LK for a short time), but Express left the local bus service market to others until deregulation in 1986 when it became a major player in bidding for tendered Gwynedd County Council mileage. Ageing Bristol VRT3 double-deckers and RE saloons were its weapons of choice in the new free-for-all.

Robert Hughes Jones retired in September 1977 and sold the company to EW and JA Jones. Under their proprietorship Express continues to prosper, both as a coach operator and as an important provider of tendered services with Optare Solos and other low-floor vehicles. In November 2010 the local public transport story came full circle when Silver Star decided to give up its local bus services, including those acquired in October 1970, and sold them to....Express Motors. Owen William Owen would probably have chuckled at that ironic twist of fate, just over a century after the start of his ground-breaking service. The route to Caernarvon had come back to its original operator after 40 years in the hands of one of his fiercest rivals.

Penmaenmawr Motor Co

The small resort town of Penmaenmawr is situated between Conway and Bangor at a point where the narrow coastal strip is punctuated by two rocky headlands jutting into the Irish Sea. The resort lies between the two and is named after the largest of the pair. Before the advent of tourism in the Victorian era it was little more than a village, the local economy dominated by the stone and slate quarries which provided most of the residents with their income. The (predictably English) Darbishire family were the most prominent among the quarry owners and were also instrumental in developing the village into a seaside resort.

In many ways the history of Penmaenmawr was similar to that of neighbouring (but much larger) Llandudno, but whereas the 'Queen of North Wales Resorts' had the Great Orme as its major natural attraction, Penmaenmawr had the Fairy Glen, a delightful wooded valley which featured an impressive waterfall. This feature was located a few miles to the east of the resort, close to the inland village of Dwygyfylchi. The best attempt that my old English tongue can make in pronouncing this is something like 'Dooeyguvulki' which may cause some amusement amongst Welsh speakers. I will not be the first to fall at this linguistic hurdle. A hotel and a cafeteria were established at the entrance to the valley and both were well-patronised by tourists staying in Penmaenmawr.

As far as can be ascertained, the traffic to the Fairy Glen was catered for by horse-drawn carriages until the start of the First World War, but with the end of that conflict several local entrepreneurs began to offer motorised conveyances on the route. In December 1919 the Penmaenmawr Motor Company was formed at a meeting held in the Bron Eryri Hotel, originally to offer an on demand taxi service to various local tourist attractions, and in July 1921 the company began a timetabled service to the Glen using a 14-seat Ford Model T registered CC 512. Competition came in the following summer season from two local garage proprietors, David Owen Davies (of Central Garage) and MB Dyson (whose family owned Dysons' Garage and also ran a clothing company which manufactured aprons and corsets in a former Methodist chapel).

While the Motor Company and the Central Garage both employed 14-seaters on the route, Mr Dyson was more ambitious and obtained a 25-seat Fiat. The larger capacity of this vehicle gave him a competitive edge and in April 1923 he acquired the Motor Company from its original owners, adopting its name for the combined operation. A 22-seat Leyland was added in July of that year, replacing the inherited Ford, and another followed for the 1924 season. At around this time the Motor Company began to use the fleetname 'Crimson Rambler' for its coaching activities.

Meanwhile, Mr Davies continued to compete, using his 14-seat vehicles to full advantage by offering more frequent services. In 1927 the Motor Company responded to this annoyance by purchasing two 14-seat Chevrolet LMs, with a third of the type joining the fleet in 1929. Two years later the newly established North West Traffic Commissioners granted licences to both operators.

With the protection afforded to it by formal licensing in place the Motor Company decided to modernise its fleet. In February 1932 four brand-new Bedford WLB 20-seaters replaced all of the existing stock except for the newest of the three Chevrolets. It was the final straw for Mr Davies who sold out to the Motor Company in February 1933. His own most recent vehicle, a six year old 14-seat Graham, was included in the deal and was used by the Motor Company as a 'reserve' vehicle for the remainder of the decade.

The mid-1930s saw another change of ownership when the Dyson family sold the Motor Company to Harold McLeland Wilde, one of several Penmaenmawr haulage contractors who specialised in quarry work. It should perhaps be noted that his surname appears as 'Wild' in many official documents, but three separate local correspondents have informed me that there should be an 'e' on the end of it from their own memories of his fleet of lorries. The same sources also suggest that Mr Wilde offered char-a-banc excursions in the 1920s, but no trace has been found of any PSVs owned prior to the Motor Company purchase. An old photograph which can be sourced by typing the words 'Penmaenmawr' and 'char-a-banc' into Google creates further ambiguities which have proven impossible to resolve.

The new owner acquired a Bedford WTB coach with a Duple 26-seat body in June 1935 and began to expand the company's private-hire

The collapse of Basil Williams' Hants & Sussex conglomerate brought many recent vintage buses and coaches onto the market in the mid-1950s. Bedford OB/Duple Mk IV service bus GOU 888 passed to the Penmaenmawr Motor Co in March 1955 and is seen here parked outside the operator's Bangor Road premises. The vehicle was replaced by the Nimbus shown in the next photograph and withdrawn from use in June 1961. *(Roy Marshall)*

Albion NS3N Nimbus 548 NLG was originally equipped with a 31-seat Willowbrook bus body and is said to have served as a demonstrator before sale to the Penmaenmawr Motor Co in October 1960. As Albion were based in Glasgow, Leyland (their parent company) in Lancashire, Willowbrook in Leicestershire, and the PMC in Caernarvonshire, the reason for the Cheshire registration is a mystery which has never been solved. The vehicle is seen here, shortly after delivery, at the Fairy Glen terminus showing 'Local Service 208'. Presumably the driver had seen Purple Motors vehicles in Bangor showing '207 Bethesda' and had decided to imitate them. Count the number of side windows and then compare this photograph to the one in the colour section! *(Roy Marshall via Lawrence Corrieri)*

Leyland KPZ2 Cub HL 7538 was already 13 years old when West Riding sold it to Pritchard of Newborough in June 1949. Its Roe bus bodywork had originally held 20 passengers but at some point during the Second World War had been 'upseated' to carry 26. The vehicle is seen in Llangefni on Pritchard's market-day service in November 1966 when it had already passed its 30th birthday. It continued in service until the following year and was then sold to Hollis of Queensferry for use on 'heritage' work. It is now preserved in Pritchard's blue and cream livery. *(Nick Craig)*

Pritchard's EY 7786 was a Bedford OWB utility bus with a post-war Mulliner body. New to Jones of Menai Bridge, it was sold to the Royal Artillery in July 1954 and used for personnel transport at Ty Croes. Pritchard bought it from its military owners in September 1960, and the vehicle is seen here in its original home town of Menai Bridge in December 1966. *(Nick Craig)*

and excursion work. Two similar machines (but with Thurgood bodywork) arrived in July 1939 but further expansion was prevented by Hitler's invasion of Poland two months later. In July 1940 the two most recent vehicles were requisitioned by the government for use as ambulances in blitz stricken Liverpool and never returned.

Although tourism evaporated with the outbreak of war, the service to the growing village of Dwygyfylchi continued for the benefit of local residents and the remaining five Bedfords were also used on military private-hire work. When peace eventually came Mr Wilde was anxious to revive the coaching part of his business, and in the summer of 1947 two Thurgood-bodied Bedford OB coaches arrived to replace the vehicles lost in 1940. A third example arrived in April 1949, on this occasion a fully-fronted machine with Plaxton bodywork acquired second-hand from Ellis Blue of Llanllechid. The third OB replaced a pre-war WLB, while a fourth OB (with Duple Vista bodywork) replaced two more of them in March 1950. This latter machine is now preserved.

Mr Wilde was a cautious man, and his first Bedford SB/Duple coach did not arrive until March 1955 – a second-hand example which replaced the 1950 OB. The SB stayed at Penmaenmawr for just over a year and was then itself replaced by a brand-new example, also with Duple bodywork. Further examples of this combination refreshed the coaching fleet on an annual basis from 1958 until 1962. While the SBs handled the company's excursion traffic the remaining OBs were dedicated to the stage carriage route and another example (with 30-seat bus bodywork by Duple) was acquired from the liquidators of Hants & Sussex, also in March 1955. It replaced the last WLB.

Like many small operators the Motor Company depended upon part-time drivers. Several of them also drove lorries for Mr Wilde's haulage firm, but others had full-time jobs elsewhere. Perhaps the most well-known of them in the 1950s was Norman Hughes ('Norman Bws') who also worked for the RAC as their local motorcycle patrol officer. His ability to mend broken vehicles made him a popular member of staff on the Fairy Glen service.

A second-hand Commer Avenger with Churchill bodywork was a surprising acquisition (from Royal Red of Llandudno) in June 1959, but the following year brought an even more surprising vehicle into the fleet. This was 548 NLG, an Albion Nimbus with a 31-seat bus body built by Willowbrook, first registered to a Cheshire dealership after a brief period of employment as a demonstrator wearing trade-plates. It replaced the bus-bodied OB, leaving the fully-fronted Plaxton coach as the only surviving OB in the fleet.

Coach deliveries during the 1960s were of further Bedford SBs, including an example with Duple (Northern) Firefly bodywork in 1964, 52-seat Bedford VALs, and a 45-seat VAM. Of much greater interest was Mr Wilde's decision to lengthen the Nimbus, inserting an extra window on each side and installing four extra seats. This appears to have been done by the Motor Company itself, an enormous challenge for such a small operator. Unfortunately, although the lengthened bodywork improved the vehicle's appearance and seating capacity, it did nothing to improve the lacklustre performance of its engine and the extra weight resulted in a snail-like ascent of gradients when fully loaded. I rode up to the Fairy Glen on this vehicle in the summer of 1969 and several ramblers (complete with rucksacks) passed by at a greater speed as it crawled up the hill. We caught up with them on the flat bits. In December 1969 the Nimbus was withdrawn and its position on the stage service was taken by a 35-seat Bristol SC4LK bus acquired from the Lincolnshire Road Car Co. This was also a sluggish performer on hills.

The subsequent fate of the Nimbus remains a mystery which has proven to be impossible to solve. The last note of it in PSV Circle records refers to its withdrawal in December 1969. However a photograph of the vehicle, in its full PMC dark blue and silver-grey livery exists (and is accessible on-line), which shows it passing a Crosville MW in full NBC leaf green and white. The NBC liveries were, of course, introduced in 1972! Despite consulting all available sources, and those of many of my correspondents, nothing has come to light to explain this anomaly.

In the following decade two disasters struck the company in quick succession. The first was the death of Mr Wilde. His widow sold the SC4LK in October 1973 but decided to keep the excursions and private-hire side of the company, along with a weekly 'shoppers express' service to Manchester developed during the 1960s. The remainder of her late husband's operations, including the 'HM Wilde' haulage business and the stage carriage service to Fairy Glen, were sold in the summer of 1974 to a new entity known as Tympan (Haulage) Ltd. Tympans were a form of slate produced in the local quarries for use in the printing industry. The directors of this new business were John Bellis (a local solicitor), Kenneth Ives (proprietor of the Puffin Hotel), and Mr JD Thomas (another Penmaenmawr haulage contractor specialising in quarrying work). The new owners used the fleetname of 'Bus Bach Motors' for their stage carriage operation. Bws Bach (with a 'w rather than a 'u') is Welsh for little bus.

The second catastrophe followed in short order when the owners of the Fairy Glen tourist attraction decided to close it, at a stroke eliminating the stage carriage route's main source of traffic. The directors of Tympan pointed this out to the Traffic Commissioners and as a result were granted licences to operate beyond Dwygyfylchi, through the scenic Sychnant Pass, to Conway. They also acquired another stage carriage service in the Conway valley, recently abandoned by Crosville, in an attempt to bolster the revenues of the PSV side of the business. Inevitably, given the primarily 'haulage' nature of Tympan, only so much time and money could be devoted to the continued existence of the struggling bus services. By the end of 1978 Kenneth Ives had taken sole ownership of the 'Bus Bach' operation and continued as its proprietor until July 1981. At that point the bus company ceased to trade, with its remaining services passing to EM Roberts of Llanddoged in the Conway valley.

Mrs EH Wilde had died in the late 1970s and the original Penmaenmawr Motor Company had closed down before its offspring. The business' famously ramshackle premises in Bangor Road survive, at one time in use by a tyre company, but the reason to go there has gone unless you need tyres. The Fairy Glen is still there too, but now on very private property and inaccessible to all but its (absentee) owners and their personal guests. This is probably the most tragic part of the story. It is a truly magical place, the kind that fires the imagination and touches the heart. And on a moonlit night you might still catch the sound of a Bedford OB or an Albion Nimbus in the distance.

Pritchard of Newborough

In normal circumstances a small coach operator with one (Thursday only) stage carriage service might not have been considered important enough to merit its own entry in this book. Pritchard of Newborough, however, was abnormal in so many fascinating ways.

Its founder and perennial proprietor, Edward Pritchard, was already 45 years old at the time of the 1930 Road Traffic Act. At that point he was one of a dozen or so independent operators providing stage services on the island of Anglesey. Twenty years later he was the only survivor of that group, the remainder having been swallowed up by Crosville or driven out of business for their refusal to sell. Pritchard was still at the wheel of his favourite bus at the age of 82 and the bus in question, a 1936 vintage Leyland Cub, had itself passed its 30th birthday by then. It hardly needs to be said that the vehicle was the last of its type in regular revenue earning service in Great Britain, or perhaps anywhere in the world. Its octogenarian owner finally withdrew it in 1967 and sold it to a preservationist. He also gave up driving PSVs in that year, although six years later he was to have one final turn at the Cub's wheel during a vintage bus rally.

The one thing that Edward Pritchard refused to do (other than sell out to Crosville) was to retire. He stayed on as the proprietor of his microcosmic bus company until the age of 99, received his telegram from the Queen in the following year, and finally passed away shortly after deregulation in 1986. The Cub is a mere youngster by comparison and is still active, painted in Pritchard's blue livery as a mechanical monument to his long and inspiring life.

Newborough is a large village in the southwest corner of Anglesey with a population of around 2,000 people. Pritchard's market-day service ran to Llangefni in the centre of the island and, given the modest size of that market town, was inexplicably popular. On some occasions in the 1950s up to three vehicles were required to satisfy demand. The company also operated a schools service to Menai Bridge (the last regular duty for the Cub), a few works contracts, and private-hires.

The beginnings of the business are lost in the mists of antiquity. The first known vehicle, a 14-seat Ford Model T registered EY 304, was

Leyland TD7c Titan BBN 196 began its career as a Massey-bodied double-decker with Bolton Corporation in 1941, one of a batch 'unfrozen' by the government after construction had been suspended at the outbreak of war. Bolton were never too happy with these 'war babies' and withdrew the machine in 1948. It then went to a dealer who removed the Massey body and sent it to Withnell of Queensferry to be rebodied as a 33-seat coach. Pritchard bought it in its new form in June 1950, and it is seen here at Menai Bridge in December 1966. *(Nick Craig)*

Also at Menai Bridge, but exactly a year later, is Guy Arab LUF/Weymann Hermes bus SPT 65. New to Northern General as fleet number 1665, it was sold to Pritchard in September 1966 and retained its previous operator's red and cream livery. Pritchard fleetnames were added at a later date. The vehicle remained in service until 1984 and was then sold for preservation in its native North East. *(Nick Craig)*

Guy Arab III/ Massey 56-seater JC 8427 was Purple Motors' first ever double-decker when delivered in June 1947. It was to remain as their only example for almost twenty years until its sale to Edde of Dunstable in July 1966, and was (effectively) replaced by Deiniolen Motors' Crossley. *(DJ Stanier)*

As with the Deiniolen Motors Bedford illustrated previously, this Purple Motors machine (JC 7734) was frequently recorded as a wartime OWB but was first registered in November 1946 and is believed to be an OB with Duple Mk II bodywork. *(DJ Stanier)*

replaced by a similarly sized second-hand REO in March 1934. In 1937 Pritchard bought three second-hand examples of the Star Flyer to join the REO. A second REO, this time a 20-seater, was acquired in November 1940. The only other wartime delivery was of an ageing PLSC3 Lion in November 1943. This 32-seater was made necessary by Pritchard's allocation of a contract for a wartime works service from the southwest of the island to the Saunders' flying-boat factory at Beaumaris.

An unusual post-war arrival was another Star Flyer, a rare sight by October 1945. It replaced one of the three bought previously. In March 1948 the 'age profile' of the fleet improved considerably when a brand-new Bedford OB/ Mulliner bus was delivered. It was to prove a one-off extravagance. In 1949 the older of the two REOs and the three Star Flyers were replaced by two Roe-bodied Leyland Cubs bought from West Riding, the aforementioned 1936 machine and a 1939 example which was retired in 1962 and is also preserved. A year later the surviving REO was replaced by a pre-war Leyland TD7c double-decker chassis (new to Bolton Corporation) which had been fitted with a post-war coach body built by Withnell of Queensferry. Two second-hand Duple-bodied Bedford OBs were acquired in the 1950s, a bus version from Mexborough & Swinton and a Vista coach from Wallace Arnold. Pritchard liked things from Yorkshire with the notable exception of anything called Crosland Taylor.

In November 1958 the company acquired its first and only Foden, a fourth-hand PVSC6 with a Plaxton coach body (registered KFM 1) which has also been preserved for posterity, while 1960 saw the acquisition of a wartime Bedford OWB which had been rebodied by Mulliner after the war. It came from the Royal Artillery and had a very low mileage for its age. Other purchases during the 1960s were mainly pre-owned Bedford SB coaches, but in September 1966 Pritchard surprised enthusiasts again by acquiring his first underfloor-engined vehicle, a Guy Arab LUF/ Weymann Hermes service bus which came from Northern General. All of the company's earlier vehicles had been painted in various combinations of dark blue and cream, but the Arab LUF remained in its previous owner's red and cream livery with Pritchard fleetnames added. It became

the regular vehicle on the route to Llangefni and remained in service until 1984, when it was 29 years old. An eager preservationist gave it a new home.

Edward Pritchard was a modest but very capable man, and well-liked in his home village where many people still reminisce about their long-lived local bus operator. I briefly encountered him in August 1966, when he was 81 and I was a lad of 13 with a Kodak Instamatic camera pointed at his Leyland Cub. At that moment the vehicle was in Menai Bridge, parked alongside a factory building. Its ancient driver shook his head and came to the door of his bus, making me fear that I was about to be told off. Instead he shouted 'It's in the shade, let me move it forward a bit'. And he did. Three days later I managed to leave the camera, with the film still inside it, on a North Western Y type bound for Derby and nobody handed it in to lost property. The picture survives, however, vividly burned into my memory to the present day.

Purple Motors of Bethesda

The quarrying community of Bethesda is set amid the Snowdonian foothills, six miles to the south of the coastal city of Bangor. Originally a group of adjacent villages which gradually merged into a single entity, the combined community took its name from the Bethesda Chapel at its geographical centre. Many of its residents use the colloquialism of 'Pesda' to refer to the larger village and prefer to describe themselves as coming from one of the original districts.

Both stone and slate are extracted from the local quarries, the purple slate from the Penrhyn site being one of the area's distinctive products. So when Thomas John Roberts started a motor-bus service from Bethesda to Bangor (by two different routes) in 1914, the trading name of Purple Motors must have appeared to be an obvious choice. The company's vehicles were never actually painted in a purple colour scheme, the dominant shade in the livery remaining a dark red – usually described as 'ruby' – throughout the company's existence. The Bangor services were also an element of continuity for more than 80 years along with a works service from Glasinfryn to Penrhyn quarry. The only other stage carriage operation, a market-day service from Bethesda to Llanrwst via Capel Curig and Bettws-y-Coed (operated on alternate weeks by Purple and Crosville), proved to be slightly more ephemeral as Purple's share was ceded to the larger company during the 1950s.

No record can be found of Purple's earliest rolling stock, but a second-hand 14-seat Ford Model T was acquired in July 1921, followed by a new example in August 1922. An Overland was also operated at some point, and possibly a REO, before three 14-seat Chevrolets arrived in 1926/7. Six years later the Chevrolets were replaced by two 20-seat Bedford WLBs, with a third new Bedford arriving in 1935 and a fourth (second-hand) in 1936. A larger 26-seat WTB bus with Duple bodywork was delivered in 1937 to supplement the WLBs on the stage services, and in 1938 two brand-new 25-seat WTB/Duple coaches arrived to promote private-hire work and excursions. Two more WTBs, a bus and a coach, were bought on the second-hand market before the beginning of the Second World War, taking the fleet strength to nine vehicles.

The founder died in January 1941 and the proprietorship passed to his widow, Mrs CJ Roberts. The pre-war Bedfords soldiered on and their ranks were refreshed by the addition of a 32-seat OWB utility bus in 1944. By the end of the war the ageing WLBs were in desperate need of replacement (although two of them carried on to work for other operators in Montgomeryshire) and four brand-new vehicles were delivered in 1947. Three of them were Bedford OBs (two Mulliner-bodied buses and a Duple Vista coach) but the fourth machine was Purple's first double-decker, a Massey-bodied Guy Arab III. With the stage carriage fleet handsomely renewed the company turned its attention to further coaches in 1948/9, acquiring a second new OB/Vista and new examples of the Crossley SD42 and Leyland PS1 Tiger, both with 33-seat Burlingham bodywork. Second-hand acquisitions in 1949/50 were of a pre-war Tiger coach, rebodied after the war by a dealership, a TS8 Tiger/Burlingham bus from Ribble, and a 1948 PS1 Tiger/Harrington coach which came from Gliderways in November 1950.

In late 1952 Mrs CJ Roberts also died and control of Purple Motors passed to the administrator of her estate, Mrs Ellen Rosina Pritchard, the deceased proprietors' daughter. Mrs Pritchard had no wish to run the business on a day-to-day basis and came to an agreement with Tom Davies of Deiniolen Motors (qv) whereby he would manage the business on her behalf in exchange for Deiniolen's vehicles being granted free access to Purple's engineering facilities at Castle Garage, Bethesda.

One change was immediately noticeable. The majority of vehicles operated since 1914 had been new, whilst all of the vehicles bought from 1952 to 1957 were second-hand. These included another Tiger/Harrington coach from Gliderways (Tom Davies took another from the same batch for Deiniolen), an OB/Duple bus from the defunct Hants & Sussex group, a 1936 vintage TS6c Tiger bus from St Helens (rebodied by Roe in 1949 and sold to Purple in 1954), and a rebodied wartime OWB. Another economical update saw the PS1 Tiger acquired from Gliderways in 1950 receiving a new coach body from Duple, to the 'Super Vega lookalike' design then on offer for half-cab chassis.

By 1958 the remainder of the coach fleet was beginning to look rather antiquated and brand-new Bedford SBs with 'genuine' Duple Super Vega bodywork were acquired in 1958, 1960, 1961, and 1962 to correct the situation. The stage carriage side of the business had to make do with further second-hand vehicles, including a PS1/Northern Coach Builders bus acquired from Stratford Blue in February 1959 and a Duple-bodied AEC Regal bus which came from Thames Valley in December 1960. The latter machine was one of a pair acquired by Tom Davies, with the other going to Deiniolen Motors. Purple's first AEC Reliance arrived in October 1963, a Duple Britannia-bodied coach which came from Monks of Leigh. It spent much of its time as a reserve vehicle on the Bangor services or on schools contracts.

An interesting purchase in January 1964 was a 30-seat Bedford C5Z1/Duple (Midland) bus which came from Hutchison of Overtown in Lanarkshire. Two months later the Deiniolen Motors (ex-Thames Valley) Regal/Duple bus was transferred into Purple Motors' ownership. Another brand-new SB/Duple coach was acquired in April 1965, carrying the Bella Vega design of bodywork which had replaced the Super Vega in 1963 as the standard Hendon offering. It was followed into the Purple fleet by three more second-hand vehicles, an SB5/Duple (Midland)

When new to Gliderways of Smethwick in 1948 this PS1 Tiger, LHA 221, was fitted with a 33-seat half-cab coach body built by Harrington. It came to Purple Motors in its original configuration in November 1950, but in the mid-1950s was rebodied with this fully-fronted 35-seat Duple unit of the 'Super Vega lookalike' design. The investment was apparently worthwhile as the vehicle was still in use in the early 1970s. *(Nick Craig)*

Purple was another operator to try a former Stratford Blue PS1 Tiger/NCB bus, in this case GUE 247 which arrived from its original home in February 1959. It is seen here in Bethesda with Purple's garage visible in the background. *(Nick Craig)*

Purple Motors' first diesel-engined Bedford arrived in January 1961 in the form of this SB1 coach with Duple Super Vega bodywork. JCC 850 is seen at the Bethesda depot, awaiting a private-hire duty, at an unknown point in the 1960s. *(Nick Craig)*

From 1959 onwards the Duple Britannia body for underfloor-engined coaches was redesigned to incorporate many of the components used in the contemporary Super Vega model. FHF 833 had been new to Wilkinson of Wallasey in 1959, later passing to Monks of Leigh and from them to Purple Motors in October 1963. It is seen here in Bethesda in March 1965. *(Nick Craig)*

bus from Clark of Consett in January 1966, a Reliance/Park Royal bus from Yorkshire Woollen District in June 1968, and a Bedford VAL14/Plaxton coach from the Penmaenmawr Motor Co six months later. The VAL was Purple's first 36ft long vehicle.

Purple's only double-decker, the 1947 Arab III, was sold in 1966 but after its departure the Tom Davies connection resulted in frequent appearances of Deiniolen's Crossley DD42, operating 'on hire' to Purple Motors on the Bethesda to Bangor routes. The legally required window stickers were not always in evidence although the vehicle remained in Deiniolen's ownership throughout its life.

The 1970s began with the arrival of a (cheap for a good reason) Bristol SC4LK/ECW bus from Thames Valley. In 1971 this appalling excuse for a PSV was followed by a Tiger Cub/Saunders-Roe bus which had been new to Sunderland District, but arrived at Bethesda from Express Motors of Rhostryfan (qv) which had just sold its own stage carriage services to Silver Star. A second Tiger Cub, but with Willowbrook dual-purpose bodywork, came from Trent in 1972. An identical vehicle was acquired by Deiniolen.

By 1976 the Duple (Midland) bus design for the Bedford SB chassis was well past its sell by date, with most operators having preferred its VAM and then Y series successors for a decade. The final few were sold off at bargain prices and one was snapped up by Purple Motors. In contrast the following year's two bus purchases were (probably) cheaper, (definitely) older, and (arguably) provided a more comfortable ride. One was a Willowbrook-bodied AEC Reliance, once a member of North Western's famous 'Black Top' dual-purpose fleet, the other an East Lancs-bodied Tiger Cub which had been new to Lancaster Corporation. Both were bought from Chester City Transport, giving them the added advantage of requiring no repaint as Chester used a shade of dark red very similar to that employed by Purple.

In 1980 Crosville withdrew from its competing services between the Bethesda area and Bangor, acquired with the business of 'Bethesda Greys' in January 1932. Purple responded by increasing its frequencies and buying its second double-decker, 14 years after selling its Arab III. The new flagship of the bus fleet was a DMS class Daimler Fleetline, cast off by London Transport when

only seven years old as they apparently lacked the engineering know-how to keep such perfectly serviceable vehicles on the road. It was the first of its kind to enter stage carriage service with a North Wales operator.

Another important change took place at around the same time when Mrs Pritchard (on behalf of the CJ Roberts estate) agreed to sell the business to a new partnership of herself, Tom Davies (as managing director), Mrs E Davies and Mrs M Williams. Given Tom Davies' other commitments to Deiniolen Motors, Stephen Bright was appointed as Purple's general manager, in charge of the daily administration of the business. The partnership arrangement established a stronger financial position, and in 1981 the company acquired a brand-new 53-seat Bedford YMT/Duple Dominant bus to help cope with the increase in traffic. The new arrival was among the first of Purple's vehicles to carry bilingual fleetnames ('Purple Motors/Moduron Porffor') which soon appeared on the remainder of the rolling stock.

A second-hand PSU3 Leopard (also with Duple Dominant bus bodywork) was acquired from Safeguard of Guildford in 1982. It was followed by a shorter PSU4 Leopard with Northern Counties bodywork bought from Chester and saving more unnecessary expenditure on paint. Deiniolen acquired an identical Chester PSU4 at the same time. This modernisation of the Purple fleet was undoubtedly a strategic decision and a wise one, as the Thatcher government was already committed to allow fresh competition in the local bus service arena. It seemed certain that the Bethesda services would attract new competitors to replace the departed Crosville.

Post-deregulation vehicles of interest were two more PSU3 Leopard/Duple Dominant buses, in this case acquired from the ever helpful Chester City Transport in 1987, and the company's third double-decker, a 1976 vintage Ailsa bought from Tayside in 1989 which replaced the DMS Fleetline. Purple also dabbled with rebodying, having the Northern Counties body removed from its PSU4 Leopard and replaced by a new Willowbrook Warrior unit in 1991.

In 1994 the existing partners decided to retire and offered the business to general manager Stephen Bright and his family. The new proprietors' period of ownership was relatively brief. In August 1998 they sold the company to Arriva Cymru and Purple Motors gradually disappeared after more than 84 years of service to the local community. It left behind it the greatest asset a defunct operator can still possess – a treasure trove of fond memories, both in Bethesda and well beyond.

Silver Star of Upper Llandwrog

The main road from Caernarvon to Pwllheli passes through Bontnewydd, and just to the south of this village a selection of minor roads leading eastwards offer access to the communities in the Snowdonian foothills including Rhostryfan, Rhosgadfan, and the parish of Upper Llandwrog which encompasses the hamlet of Cesarea (now known as Y Fron). The vehicles of the Clynnog & Trevor Motor Co have always ignored these turnings, being more intent upon their home territory on the Lleyn peninsula.

Quarrying and farming were the traditional local industries in these highland villages, and in the late 19th and early 20th centuries a narrow-gauge railway provided them with a lifeline to the rest of the country. The railway ceased to carry passengers in 1916 and had vanished completely by 1922. By then the villages were well provided with bus services by no fewer than six competing operators.

One of these was Owen W Owen's Express Motors of Rhostryfan (qv), the pioneering bus operator in the area, which had started a timetabled (albeit Saturday only) service in 1909. The others included Owen E Hughes, trading as Mountaineer, and a confusing array of proprietors who shared the surname of Jones although they were not (as far as can be ascertained) that closely related. Fleetnames were obviously required to differentiate between them. Hugh Jones traded as Tait Motors, David Jones as Dixie Bus Service, Michael Jones (of Tryfan Range Garage) as Tryfan Ranger, and John Ivor Jones (of Upper Llandwrog/Cesarea) as the Silver Star Service. Despite this plethora of competing Joneses attempting to keep up with each other, business was apparently brisk, as all survived to be licensed by the Traffic Commissioners in 1931/2 and all but one (Tait) were still trading in 1945.

John Ivor Jones bought his first motor vehicle, believed to be a Ford Model T lorry-bus, in May 1918 and initially operated 'upon demand'

although it could be guaranteed that the Ford would make several trips to Caernarvon each Saturday. A timetabled service followed in late 1920. Details of the early fleet remain elusive, but in March 1929 Mr Jones acquired a one year old 20-seat Guy (UN 2153) from an operator in Denbighshire. A similar machine originally owned by Hayton of Carlisle (HH 4980) was acquired from Ribble in late 1931. The two Guys were followed by a 20-seat Commer 6TK/Willowbrook coach in 1936. This bore the Warwickshire registration WD 1917 but had later served with Mechell Maroon of Anglesey before passing to Crosville in 1935. Crosville had no use for such vehicles and sold it to a local dealer.

By the end of 1937 the two Guys had been retired, replaced by a pair of Bedford WLBs acquired from Williams of Llithfaen (qv) and Yates of Runcorn. Another acquisition at this time was a Ford AA 20-seater (VB 8333) which had been new to Dawson of Croydon in 1930. The ex-Williams WLB was sold in July 1939 leaving Silver Star with a fleet of one Bedford, one Commer, and one Ford when war began in September.

According to some sources Mr Jones agreed to sell the company to the Thomas family (also of Upper Llandwrog) in 1941, but if this is correct the actual sale was delayed for several years as he remained the proprietor of record until October 1949. Meanwhile, the Ford and the Commer were sold, leaving the ex-Yates WLB as the company's solitary vehicle. In December 1946 this too departed, replaced by another WLB (BYL 156) which had been new to the British School of Motoring in London and then served with two operators in East Anglia before migrating to North Wales.

Tait Motors had already gone and the number of competing firms was about to be reduced still further. In 1947 Mountaineer and Express were combined under the latter's name, and in July 1948 the Dixie Bus Service's final vehicle (a 1938 Dodge SBF) was also sold to the enlarged Express Motors operation. To many observers it seemed that Silver Star would be the next to disappear, but Mr Jones (and his heir apparent Edward William Thomas) rose to the challenge. In November 1948 the pre-war WLB was retired and replaced by a 32-seat Bedford OWB utility bus acquired from Mid-Wales Motorways. A year later, shortly

Before the introduction of the VAS range in 1962 Bedford's contender in the 29/30 seat market was the C5 series. This C5Z1 model, SVA 438, had been built to the order of Lanarkshire operator Hutchison of Overtown and carried a 30-seat Duple (Midland) bus body. Purple Motors bought it in January 1964 and kept it until January 1977, so most of its working life was spent in the Bangor area. *(Nick Craig)*

In December 1960 Tom Davies bought two Duple-bodied AEC Regal buses from a dealer, one for his own Deiniolen Motors fleet (DMO 320) and one for Purple Motors (DMO 326). Both had started life with Newbury & District in 1947 as rear entrance 35-seaters, had passed to Thames Valley in 1950, and had been rebuilt as forward entrance 34-seaters in 1958. Purple's DMO 326 was withdrawn from use during 1964 and replaced by DMO 320 which was transferred into the ownership of the Bethesda based company (as seen here) in March of that year. *(TG Turner)*

Bedford SB5/Duple Bella Vega coach BCC 286C was new to Purple Motors in April 1965 and became the new flagship of the company's small coaching fleet. *(Nick Craig)*

WTY 906 was an SB5 with a 42-seat Duple (Midland) bus body, new to Armstrong of Westerhope in Northumberland in 1962. It then moved south to serve with Clark of Consett in County Durham, and in January 1966 was acquired by Purple Motors. The vehicle is seen here at the Bangor (Town Clock) terminus two months later. *(Nick Craig)*

after the official change of ownership, the OWB was joined by Silver Star's first ever brand-new vehicle, an Austin CXB with 29-seat coach bodywork by Mann Egerton.

This was a daring move by a company which had almost faded away, but Mr Thomas's next acquisition was even more audacious. In April 1953 Silver Star acquired the business of Tryfan Ranger from Mr MB Jones along with a second route to Caernarvon and four Bedfords; a pre-war WTB coach, two OWB utility buses, and a post-war OB/Duple Vista coach. The Silver Star fleet went from two vehicles to six, while the six original competitors had now become just two, a rationalisation which helped to ensure the survival of both Silver Star and Express Motors as the private family car became their common enemy.

Soon after the Tryfan Ranger take-over the company's purchasing policy switched from Bedfords to good quality 'heavyweight' chassis with various models of Leyland's front-engined Tiger being particularly favoured. The first was a pre-war TS8/Duple coach acquired from WC Standerwick in May 1955, quickly followed by two TS8/ECW buses from Maidstone & District. The next Leyland was a TD5, rebodied as a single-decker coach by Harrington after the war, which came from The Creams of Llandudno in May 1959, while a TS7 bus (from Lincolnshire Road Car Co) was added in December of that year. One odd man out, arriving in July 1961, was a Weymann-bodied Bristol L5G bus which came from North Western. This was the first Bristol vehicle in the Silver Star fleet but proved to be the forerunner of many more over the next five decades.

Post-war Leylands made their debut in September 1961 with the acquisition of a PS1 Tiger/Roe bus from Lancashire United Transport. A second PS1, but with a fully-fronted coach body built by Duple, came from Lewis of Greenwich in May 1962. The next purchase was the company's second Bristol, a 35-seat SC4LK bus acquired from Eastern National in July 1964. It replaced the last of the pre-war Tigers, although lamentably underpowered in comparison.

The coaching side of the company was finally rejuvenated in July 1965, by the addition of a two year old Bedford SB5/Duple Bella Vega from Milburn of Anglesey which dislodged the fully-fronted PS1 Tiger onto stage carriage work. Another coach, although specifically purchased for use on the bus services, came in June 1966 in the shape of a Commer-Beadle T48 from Devon General. Several of these raucous two-stroke machines found their way from Devonshire to North Wales operators. Silver Star's was registered XTA 848, while identical twin XTA 849 also ran into Caernarvon with Clynnog & Trevor who would go on to buy three bus-bodied versions of the same combination from Devon General. Another of the coaches, XTA 847, went to an Anglesey private-hire operator. This sudden influx of T48s reminded many enthusiasts of the quartet of ex-LUT PS1 Tiger/Roe buses which had invaded the Caernarvon area in 1961; JTJ 91 and 96 working for Express Motors, JTJ 97 for Whiteway, and JTJ 98 for Silver Star.

Another (third-hand) Bristol SC4LK bus replaced the ex-North Western L5G in November 1967. As Crosville had already discovered, the SC4LK might well be a gutless, noisy, and unpleasant creature, but it was also very economical. Younger readers should imagine an Optare Solo-sized vehicle made by the least talented team in an episode of 'Scrapheap Challenge'. Silver Star's neighbours at Express Motors were also impressed by the low purchase price and low fuel consumption of the SC4LK and bought two of their own from Thames Valley in February 1970.

Express's tenure as an operator of SC4LKs on local bus services was to prove extremely brief. In October 1970 company proprietor Robert Hughes Jones decided to sell the stage carriage side of his business to Silver Star. The deal included one of his SC4LKs (the other was retained for a schools contract) and two more elderly front-engined Bristols. One of these was an L6A/ECW bus which Crosville had converted from rear entrance to forward entrance, to make it marginally acceptable as a driver-only vehicle. The other was a slightly longer LL5G/ECW bus similarly converted at the behest of Thames Valley but with the addition of a 'full-front' to give it a slightly unconvincing air of modernity. Express remained in business as a coach operator with a new depot at Bontnewydd, but Silver Star now had a monopoly of the diminishing stage carriage traffic in the highland villages. Six operators had finally dwindled to one.

Bristols continued to dominate the fleet during the 1970s. A fourth SC4LK, like the first two new to Eastern National but acquired from its second owner, Cumberland Motor Services, arrived in April 1971. The SC4LKs were joined by an MW/ECW bus from United Automobile Services in 1975, an RELH/ECW coach acquired from National Travel (South East) in 1978 and an MW/ECW coach from Western National in 1979. This latter duet looked quite attractive in Silver Star's mustard and cream coach livery, while even the vile SC4LKs looked better after being repainted into the company's new bus livery of two-tone blue and cream. A variety of 'pre-owned' Bedfords were also acquired during the 1970s, the most interesting among them a VAM/Strachan service bus which had been new to King Alfred in Winchester.

The new decade began with a major shock. In 1980 Silver Star purchased a 'job lot' of seven vehicles put up for auction by the South Yorkshire PTE. Four of them were AEC Reliances with 41-seat dual-purpose bodywork by Weymann, new to Maidstone & District in 1961. Sold off to Booth & Fisher in 1973, they had passed with that famous independent business to the PTE in February 1976 and four years after that became the new regulars on Silver Star's stage services. The remaining three PTE disposals were a very mixed bag made up of a late-model SB5/Plaxton coach, a Ford R1114/Duple coach (Silver Star's first Ford since VB 8333 in the 1930s), and a 25-seat Seddon Pennine IV-236 'midibus' – more usually found on city centre shuttle services than in the wilds of rural Caernarvonshire.

The Reliances (and most of the rest of the then current fleet) were soon wearing bilingual fleet-names ('Silver Star/Seren Arian'), a reflection of the growing pride taken in the Welsh language. In 1981 they were joined by another AEC, a rear-engined Swift with 42-seat bus bodywork made by Seddon's Pennine Coachcraft subsidiary. The vehicle had been ordered by Rochdale Corporation, delivered to the SELNEC PTE in 1972, and was purchased from Greater Manchester Transport. The Bristol domination of the Silver Star fleet appeared to be at an end (although a second MW bus had arrived from Lincolnshire in March 1982), but in 1985 the next generation of the marque came to the company when a 43-seat Bristol LH6L/ECW service bus was acquired. Like the Swift it had started life in Greater Manchester with the PTE,

but came to its new home in North Wales from Flora of Helston in Cornwall.

At deregulation in 1986 Silver Star registered its main services as commercial operations and also tendered for several subsidised Gwynedd County Council routes. The fleet grew rapidly as a result and most of the new arrivals were ageing Bristols with ECW bodywork, beginning with an RE with dual-purpose bodywork (new to West Yorkshire) in 1987. Three more LH service buses followed in 1989 and replaced the last of the 1961 vintage AEC Reliances which had given exceptional service to all four of their operators. The Swift also went.

In 1990 Edward William Thomas decided to retire and passed control of Silver Star to his son Elfryn. The new proprietor continued to buy Bristol LHs (including examples which had started life with London Transport and Crosville) and, to a lesser extent, REs. There was also an ex-PMT Bristol VRT3/ECW double-decker, acquired in 1992 for schools work. It was the company's first ever double-decker and stayed until 1997. More modern vehicles were purchased for tendered services, including the company's first Dennis Darts.

Elfryn Thomas was also eager to expand the company's coaching and extended tours programmes and Silver Star soon became a major force in this market alongside Caelloi Motors and Express Motors. As the new millennium progressed this became the most important source of revenue, although Silver Star continued to update its service bus fleet by replacing assorted Bristols with Mercedes minibuses. Many of the Bristols were sold to preservationists who restored them to the liveries of their original operators, and the last of the marque were retired from Silver Star's stage routes in 2006/7.

Just as the last of the older buses were going, some even older ones were arriving. In August 2009 the company began a 'heritage' operation under the name of Snowdon & Menai Strait Vintage Coach Tours. An AEC Regal III/Burlingham coach, LPT 328, which had been owned by Elfryn Thomas for several years as a preserved vehicle, was restored to 'Class VI' PCV status and put to work in harness with a PS1 Tiger/Crossley bus. The latter machine had been new to Blackburn as BCB 340 but had at some point been re-registered as EAS 956. It retained its basic

Purple's Castle Garage premises in Bethesda had only limited parking space and many vehicles were parked at the nearby Old Station Yard site. That location provides the background for DHD 194, an AEC Reliance with 43-seat bus bodywork by Park Royal to the BET Federation design. New to Yorkshire Woollen in 1958 as fleet number 814, it passed to Purple in June 1968. *(Nick Craig)*

Also at the Old Station Yard is Bristol SC4LK/ECW bus NBL 733, new to Thames Valley as fleet number 776 and sold to Purple Motors in February 1970. Express Motors received two of the same batch in the same year. Parked behind the Bristol is Deiniolen Motors' Crossley DD42 JC 9795, by then more or less a fixture on Purple's services from Bethesda rather than its own from Dinorwic. *(Nick Craig)*

The Ribble subsidiary WC Standerwick of Blackpool bought this TS8 Tiger/Duple 31-seat coach, RN 8515, in 1939 as fleet number 96. After sixteen years of service it was sold to Silver Star in May 1955 and spent another six years on that company's stage carriage routes before being retired in September 1961. It was replaced by an ex-LUT PS1 Tiger/Roe bus, JTJ 98. *(DJ Stanier)*

FKO 83 was another TS8 Tiger, but with 34-seat bus bodywork by ECW. New to Maidstone & District, it was one of a pair (the other was FKO 82) sold to Silver Star in December 1955. It lasted until February 1960 while its identical twin survived until July 1961. *(Roy Marshall via the Omnibus Society)*

The longer lived of the two ex-M&D TS8 buses was replaced in July 1961 by this Weymann-bodied Bristol L5G bus, BJA 408. As its Stockport registration suggests, it came from the North Western Road Car Co fleet. The chassis dated from 1946 and had originally been fitted with a Brush body, but in 1958 received a 1948 Weymann unit previously fitted to a pre-war vehicle. The handsome mongrel is seen at the Silver Star depot in March 1966. It was withdrawn from use during 1968. *(Nick Craig)*

Silver Star would eventually operate a total of four Bristol SC4LK/ECW 35-seat buses. The first to arrive was 610 JPU, previously fleet number 440 with Eastern National, acquired in July 1964 and seen here at the depot in October 1966. *(Nick Craig)*

This Bedford VAM5 with a 46-seat Strachan Pacemaker II bus body, EOR 415D, was new to the famous Hampshire independent King Alfred Motor Services in 1966. In April 1973 it passed with that business into the ownership of Hants & Dorset and became that company's fleet number 2501. Its stay with the NBC subsidiary was brief, however, as it was sold to a dealer in March 1974 and was then acquired by Silver Star. *(DJ Stanier)*

Despite the horrible (but irresistibly cheap) SC4LKs, Silver Star continued to have a taste for Bristols, particularly those with larger engines. This Bristol RELH6G/ECW 47-seat coach, YHK 725F, had been new to Eastern National in 1968, later passing to National Travel (South East). Silver Star bought it in May 1978 and painted it into their attractive mustard and cream coach livery. By February 1984 it had been withdrawn from use, but remained at the depot for the rest of the decade. *(DJ Stanier)*

Blackburn (green and cream) livery while the Regal III was treated to a full repaint into Silver Star's new pale green colour scheme.

Express Motors had re-entered the local bus service market with a vengeance after deregulation, operating tendered services across a wide swathe of northwestern Wales. In November 2010 Elfryn Thomas decided to concentrate on Silver Star's coaching activities and the company's local network, along with several vehicles, was sold to Express Motors. Few could have predicted the transaction, more than 40 years after Express had sold its original services to Silver Star, but it was deeply satisfying to see the routes remain in local ownership rather than in the hands of a faceless conglomerate.

Silver Star is now one of the leading coach operators in Wales, and in 2008 opened a new office in Wrexham (on the opposite side of the country) to further expand its touring programme. We must wish the company every success in the future while inevitably feeling a profound nostalgia for 'the good old days'. And who knows, in another 40 years time Express may decide to sell its local bus services to Silver Star again. Stranger things have happened!

Whiteway of Waenfawr

The Williams family owned a grocery business, known as The Liverpool House, in the small village of Waenfawr four miles to the south of Caernarvon on the Beddgelert road. Owen Robert Williams expanded the family's interests, establishing a garage and diversifying into haulage and coal deliveries. In May 1912 he added his first passenger carrying motor vehicle, a Wolseley registered CC 544 which could be fitted with up to 18 seats when not required for haulage duties.

The new machine proved to be popular with local residents. Although Caernarvon was only four miles away, in an age when most lower income people thought nothing of walking such distances, the return to the village included some very steep gradients – especially for those burdened with shopping. The First World War delayed further expansion of this side of the family's enterprises, but in 1919 Mr Williams started a timetabled service from his home village to the county town under the trading name of 'Caernarvon & Waenfawr District Motors'.

It is believed that other buses were operated in the early days of the company, but the next identifiable vehicle was CC 2422, a 32-seat Thornycroft X char-a-banc delivered in September 1920. Readers with a prior interest in Whiteway may notice that this delivery date (and some others presented here) are in conflict with those given in earlier publications, including the history of Whiteway produced by the talented local historian Bill Rear, but they are taken from Caernarvonshire motor taxation records and are therefore considered to be more precise.

The next vehicle was another Thornycroft, on this occasion s second-hand Model J acquired in 1922. It was followed in 1924 by a brand-new 26-seat Lancia Pentaiota bus, and a second (almost identical) Lancia arrived in June 1926 along with a 14-seat Chevrolet registered CC 6430. One year later a third Thornycroft was delivered in the shape of a 20-seat Model A2 with a Santus coach body registered CC 7386. A similar machine (but an A6 with London Lorries bodywork) arrived in 1928, but in 1929 Mr Williams switched his allegiance to Maudslay and received one of the new 'low floor' ML models with a 35-seat coach body by Hall Lewis of Cardiff.

Mr Williams' original stage carriage service ran from Bettws Garmon, a small hamlet a mile to the south of Waenfawr, to Caernarvon. Some journeys were extended beyond Bettws Garmon to Plas-y-Nant, a large country house which had been converted into a holiday retreat for under-privileged children by an organisation affiliated to the Methodist Church. In the early days of the route competition came from Richards (Busy Bee) of Caernarvon which ran through Waenfawr and Bettws Garmon on its way to Beddgelert and Portmadoc, but in 1925 Richards sold out to Crosville who thus established a presence in the area. Other competition came from William Samuel Jones (Brown Bus) of Beddgelert, operating from their base to Caernarvon, and from the Roberts family of Waenfawr (trading as Blue Bus) who ran a service from Ceunant to Caernarvon via their home village. Mr Williams painted his vehicles in an all-white colour scheme to make them stand out from those of Brown Bus, Blue Bus, and 'The Greys' (as Crosville's fleet were known due to their original livery).

In April 1930 Trevor Roberts of Blue Bus, probably unwilling to face the red tape of the new

Road Traffic Act, decided to sell his business to his neighbours in Waenfawr. The deal included the Ceunant route and a three year old 14-seat Chevrolet, CC 7738. Mr Williams' similar machine had already gone by this point, having been converted into a lorry and then sold. The inherited Chevrolet remained in service until August 1933 when it was replaced by a new 14-seat Austin registered JC 1285. The following year brought a much more impressive purchase in the form of JC 1952, a Leyland LT5A Lion with a 32-seat coach body by Duple. As with all previous vehicles the livery was overall white, but this new coach celebrated that fact by carrying a new fleet-name of 'Whiteway' in addition to the traditional 'Caernarvon & Waenfawr District Motors' titles. All later acquisitions would carry the new trading name with the older version being phased out as vehicles were retired.

It should perhaps be noted here that the official name of the business was OR Williams & Sons throughout its existence and that both the old and new versions of the titles painted on the vehicles were nothing more than 'branding' with no legal status. A sister company, Williams Transport Services Ltd of Caernarvon, was later formed but initially concentrated on haulage work and the maintenance of office premises in Caernarvon. In post-war years these premises would become a booking office for Whiteway's excursions, and several Whiteway PSVs would be registered to WTS for tax purposes, but the limited company had no official connection to the stage carriage services.

A new 20-seat Morris bus was delivered in 1935, but the most significant acquisitions of the mid-1930s were all 'pre-owned'. One was a Leyland TS2 Tiger with a 32-seat Ramsden coach body (VH 2067) acquired from Hanson of Huddersfield in August 1935. The other three were Maudslay ML3s which came from Cadman Services of Orrell near Wigan. Cadman had recently been acquired by Ribble, a staunch Leyland user with no place for Maudslays in its fleet. Two of these machines (TF 1914/TF 2221) had been new to Cadman and carried 32-seat bodywork by Barton & Danson. The third (SF 5913) had started life with SMT in Scotland and was equipped with a 32-seat body by Short Brothers. A fourth 'used' Maudslay (UL 8197) was also acquired but may not have been operated in service by Whiteway.

With war approaching few purchases were made in the late 1930s. A small 1934 Austin (YD 3492) came from a Somerset operator in 1937, and in the following year a Leyland KP3 Cub with a 25-seat coach body by Service (registered WJ 4039) arrived from Sheffield United Tours. The final pre-war acquisition was Whiteway's first ever Bedford, a 26-seat WTB/Duple coach (FF 5346) which came from Davies of Barmouth in the summer of 1939. The WTB was placed into storage for the duration of the war along with several other Whiteway vehicles which somehow avoided being requisitioned by the government. Meanwhile, the (much reduced) stage carriage timetable was maintained by three Maudslays and the KP3 Cub. All four vehicles survived the war, but the founder of the business sadly passed away in 1943. Control of Whiteway passed to his younger son, RG (Glyn) Williams – an older brother ran the haulage business. By early 1945 the Maudslays were in need of major refurbishment and were relieved by two OWB utility buses, one delivered new and one second-hand from Western SMT. The Scottish example, ACS 971, proved to be more of a fixture than its 'native' cousin and stayed with Whiteway until April 1957.

Like most operators the company found itself desperate for additional vehicles to meet the post-war demand. The need was made even more urgent by Whiteway's acquisition of Jones of Beddgelert (Brown Bus) in 1946. The purchase brought a new daily service from Beddgelert to Caernarvon via Bettws Garmon and Waenfawr, a Saturday only operation from Beddgelert to Nant Gwynant, and a schooldays only run from Beddgelert to Portmadoc. Jones' only active vehicle by the end of the war, an ageing Thornycroft, was also acquired but was deemed unfit for further service and replaced by a third OWB (GND 940) as a temporary measure. Other stop-gap purchases included two more pre-war Leyland Cubs, one of which was extensively rebuilt and acquired the post-war registration JC 9270.

A more drastic solution was needed to solve the capacity problem. In late 1947 one was found in the shape of four vehicles acquired from Sheffield Corporation; a Leyland TD5 double-decker with Cravens bodywork, two all-Leyland TD7c double-deckers, and a Cravens-bodied TS8 Tiger saloon. The TD5 and one of the TD7s entered service in early 1948 as Whiteway's first double-decker vehicles and replaced the remaining

TDK 547K, an AEC Swift with 41-seat Pennine bus bodywork, was ordered by Rochdale Corporation but actually delivered to the SELNEC PTE in 1972. It soon acquired Greater Manchester Transport titles and spent most of its time with the PTE in the Leigh area. In August 1981 GMT sold it to Silver Star. Seen here leaving Caernarvon with a crumpled blind and a misapplied side advertisement for 'Bus Rovers', the vehicle was replaced at the end of the 1980s by a Bristol LH6L. *(Author's Collection)*

Silver Star's first Bristol LH6L was this 43-seat 'flat fronted' ECW bus, BNE 765N. New to Greater Manchester Transport in 1974 it migrated to Richardson (Flora) of Helston in Cornwall before returning northwards to Silver Star in April 1985. Alongside it at the depot (in the mustard and cream livery) is Ford R1014/Duple Dominant coach NHL 45P, acquired from South Yorkshire PTE in 1981. *(Martyn Hearson)*

This Massey-bodied Leyland PD1 Titan, BG 9672, was new to Birkenhead Corporation in 1947 as fleet number 113. Withdrawn from use in 1960, it came to Whiteway early in the following year and lasted until 1969. *(Andrew Porter via Peter Harden)*

BG 9672 appears again in this view of Whiteway's Waenfawr depot. Parked next to it is the company's other PD1 Titan, DED 797, carrying Alexander bodywork to Leyland's own design. New to Warrington Corporation as fleet number 18 in 1946, it was acquired by Whiteway in June 1963 and gave 16 years of faithful service to its new owner. To the right of DED 797 is the rear end of Austin K8VC/Kenex 14-seater AJC 730. *(Nick Craig)*

Maudslays. Fortunately, the company had just built a new garage with 16ft high entrance doors to replace the modest 'shed' previously in use. The TS8 single-decker eventually entered service in 1949 after conversion from rear entrance to forward entrance, while the other TD7c had its double-deck body removed and replaced by the Duple coach body from the 1934 LT5A Lion. This latter vehicle had been requisitioned during the war and then returned to Whiteway in 1945 with a seized engine.

Three new Bedford OB/Duple Vista coaches were also brought into service in 1948/9, followed by a 14-seat Austin K8VC/Kenex 'bus'. The Austin, little more than a converted van (think of a 1940s version of a Sherpa/Carlyle), was bought for a new service aimed at the tourist market. This ran from Aber Shore, on the opposite side of the River Seiont from Caernarvon, to a popular beach at Y Foryd. Several journeys each day continued 'the long way' around the Seiont estuary to Castle Square in Caernarvon, and then ran (empty except for the driver) across the weight restricted swing-bridge to Aber Shore to resume the shuttle service to the beach. At times of peak demand the Austin was supplemented by a Bedford OB which had the disadvantage of being unable to use the swing-bridge, even when empty.

The fleet then settled down to a long period of stability. The final pre-war coaches were replaced by a pair of new Bedford SBG/Duple Super Vegas (delivered in 1955) and two second-hand OB/Vistas, and in 1957 an OB/Duple bus was acquired from Bristol to replace the last of the OWBs. A second OB bus (but with Beadle bodywork) came from Hants & Dorset in 1960 and the pair were usually to be found on the Beddgelert services acquired from Jones.

The ex-Sheffield TS8 was retired in September 1960, its place in the fleet taken by a post-war PS1 Tiger with a 35-seat bus body by Burlingham, previously operated by Cumberland Motor Services. It had a forward entrance and Whiteway adapted it for driver-only operation despite its half-cab layout, a conversion which had already been tried on the TD7c/Duple hybrid with passable success (although drivers with back-ache might have disagreed). This TD7c 'saloon' was retired in 1961 after another PS1 Tiger (this one with Roe bodywork and from Lancashire United Transport) received a Whiteway 'omo' conversion.

The former Sheffield double-deckers were also in desperate need of replacement by the early 1960s. The TD5 went first (in 1961), supplanted by an ex-Birkenhead PD1 Titan with Massey bodywork, while the TD7c lasted until 1963 when it was replaced by an Alexander-bodied (to Leyland's own design under licence) PD1 acquired from Warrington Corporation. The Massey-bodied machine was retired in 1969 but the Warrington vehicle endured until its 33rd birthday in 1979! Four second-hand Bedford SB coaches and an Austin J2 minibus were also acquired in the 1960s. The PS1 Tigers followed the Birkenhead PD1 into retirement in January 1970 and were replaced on the stage carriage routes by the two surviving OB/Vista coaches which howled merrily about their business until the late 1970s. They outlasted the ex-Bristol OB bus which was sold to a preservationist in 1973. The other OB bus, with its unattractive Beadle bodywork, had left the fleet in 1963.

Whiteway's bus fleet in the 1970s attracted enthusiasts from far and wide, anxious to sample the increasingly rare delights of Bedford OBs and a Leyland PD1 still in everyday passenger service (and in the context of stunningly photogenic scenery). By the end of 1979 the show was over and the veterans had been replaced by a trio of 36ft long Leyland Leopards with BET Federation style bodywork. Two were 49-seat dual-purpose variants acquired from Trent, the other a 53-seat bus from Ribble. For nearly two years there were no double-deckers in the Whiteway fleet until the arrival of a Park Royal-bodied Daimler Fleetline from West Midlands PTE. This was bought for a schools contract but could also be found on the stage services on busy summer weekends.

The Aber Shore to Y Foryd route had come to an end in 1972, after the long overdue retirement of the Austin K8VC, but partial compensation had come from a new local service in Caernarvon, from the town centre to the Hendre Park estate. At times of low demand this service was sometimes operated by Whiteway's other 1981 acquisition, at the opposite end of the scale from the Fleetline, a 12-seat Bedford CFL/Reeve Burgess minicoach. This machine was also used on the Beddgelert services outside of high season.

Whiteway survived deregulation in 1986, but faced increasing competition along the only part of its route network which was profitable on a year-round basis – the four mile sector from Waenfawr to Caernarvon. The end was almost inevitable, and in early 1989 Glyn Williams decided to close the company down. The final service from Beddgelert to Caernarvon ran in April of that year, operated by the uninspiring Bedford CFL minicoach. To some long-time Whiteway aficionados it seemed as if the company had ended with a whimper rather than a bang.

Williams of Bethesda

In October 1952 the Denbighshire operator Williams of Maerdy (see Part Two) opened a second base in Bethesda as further expansion in their sparsely populated home area had proven impossible to achieve. It is believed that Mr Williams Sr remained in Maerdy while his son oversaw the new branch in Bethesda. In April 1959 the two men decided to abandon their poorly patronised routes from Melin-y-Wig to Corwen and Ruthin to concentrate upon the Bethesda operations, although they continued to offer private-hire and other coaching services in the original area around Maerdy until 1978. A sign of Williams Coaches improving prosperity came two years after the closure of the Maerdy base in the shape of a brand-new Bedford SB1/Plaxton coach with the registration KCC 1. The plate alone would now be worth more than the vehicle itself. Subsequent acquisitions included a six year old SB5/Duple coach from Hanmer of Southsea (near Wrexham) in June 1968, and a 1968 VAM70/Duple which came from the Shearings group in November 1969.

Williams maintained a tenuous connection to its roots in the shape of an express service from the Alwen valley (to the north of Maerdy) to Wrexham, which operated on the last Monday of each month and was actually little more than a regular excursion for the benefit of those wishing to visit Wrexham market. A more serious foray back into the world of timetabled services came in May 1972 when the company introduced a market-day service from Bethesda to Llanrwst via Capel Curig and Bettws-y-Coed. This replaced Crosville's 'M99' (Capel Curig-Llanrwst) which had been withdrawn in January 1972 as part of the NBC subsidiary's rural cutbacks. A variation of the licence later allowed some journeys to run through to and from Bangor, although Purple Motors' existing traffic rights between Bangor and Bethesda were protected by local restrictions on picking up and setting down points.

In April 1973 Williams received permission to replace its Alwen valley to Wrexham express with a new stage carriage service which started at Bettws-y-Coed before proceeding to Maerdy, Corwen, and Wrexham. As with the earlier incarnation of this licence, the authorisation was for a service on the last Monday of each month. At the same time they were granted another 'shoppers' service from Bettws-y-Coed, Maerdy, and Corwen to Oswestry which operated on the second Wednesday in each month.

In February 1978 Williams sold its remaining coaching interests in the Maerdy area to FG (Fred) Owen of Corwen, although the firm continued to operate its 'shoppers' services to Wrexham and Oswestry. These finally came to an end, along with all other stage carriage operations, in July 1981 when the licences were withdrawn by the North West Traffic Commissioners. The reasons for this remain obscure, but in November 1981 the premises in Bethesda were sold to Ogwen Valley Coaches and Williams Coaches ceased to trade. It is believed that there may be a family connection between Williams of Maerdy/Bethesda and Williams of Bala, but the exact nature of this link has also proven impossible to establish from the available records.

Williams of Llithfaen

The village of Llithfaen, close to the north coast of the Lleyn peninsula, is only three miles as the crow flies from the village of Trevor – the home of the famous Clynnog & Trevor Motor Company. It would, however, be a very tired crow as it would have to fly across the looming bulk of Yr Eifl, at 1,850 feet one of the highest mountains on the peninsula. Llithfaen lies on the western flank of this impressive part of the Welsh landscape.

In the days before roads with 'all weather' surfaces, less than a century ago, Llithfaen was all but inaccessible from the outside world except by boat, on horseback, or on foot. The First World War and its aftermath led to road improvements, partly as a 'make work' scheme for those fortunate enough to return from the conflict, and Llithfaen's very first motor-bus arrived in 1920.

Despite the modest population of the village, by the end of the decade there were three bus operators in the community. Tudor Evans ran a service to the county town of Caernarvon,

JTJ 97 was one of the ex-LUT PS1 Tiger/Roe buses which invaded Caernarvonshire during 1961. Whiteway modified it to suit one man operation, but drivers disliked such conversions as the constant body swivelling involved could cause muscle pains and cramps. *(Andrew Porter via Peter Harden)*

This Burlingham-bodied PS1 Tiger bus, GAO 516, was also modified for 'driver only' operations. The vehicle had been new to Cumberland Motor Services as fleet number 256, and came to Whiteway in July 1961. It is seen at the depot alongside PD1 Titan DED 797 and Austin AJC 730. *(Nick Craig)*

MHU 50, a Bedford OB with Duple Mk IV bus bodywork, came to Whiteway from Bristol Omnibus in June 1957 and continued in service as a front-line vehicle until the early 1970s – usually on the scenic route to Beddgelert. In this view it is seen in Caernarvon next to Clynnog & Trevor's Regal III/Windover coach KWA 708 and an unidentified SB5/Duple Bella Vega. The OB was acquired for preservation (in its original Bristol livery) in 1973. *(David Cunningham)*

Ribble was the source for this 53-seat Leopard/Marshall bus, ARN 592C, acquired by Whiteway in 1979. Clynnog & Trevor bought an identical vehicle from the same batch. The Whiteway machine is seen in Castle Square, Caernarvon, with its overall whitewash relieved by Gwynedd county council insignia for 'Sherpa' services – tourist oriented routes which were subsidised by local ratepayers. *(DJ Stanier)*

while Alun Roberts (of the Eifl Garage) and Mr MJ Williams provided competing services southwards to the railhead at Pwllheli. Roberts' choice of vehicle remains unrecorded and his service had ceased to operate by 1939. Tudor Evans sold out to Crosville in 1935, contributing his Caernarvon service and a 26-seat Vickers-bodied Gilford 168SD to the English operator. The Williams family would persevere and their buses would be a familiar sight in Llithfaen and Pwllheli until Crosville had been dismembered and deregulation had become the new status quo.

The history of the Williams fleet is far from complete. In October 1925 the founder purchased a four year old Thornycroft with 28 seats (CC 3040) from the Llandudno Motor Company and this might or might not have been the original vehicle on the route. It was sold in 1927 and subsequent vehicles were registered to the founder's son, Mr MH Williams. These included a 20-seat Bedford WLB (JC 232) acquired when new in 1931 – note the four year gap between the sale of the Thornycroft and the delivery of this second identifiable vehicle – and a second-hand REO (LG 2391), also a 20-seater, which came to Llithfaen in the mid-1930s. The REO was new in 1929, so even if the date of its purchase by Williams is incorrect it cannot account for the post-Thornycroft vacuum. There were evidently other vehicles which escaped the attention of historically minded observers.

The date of the REO's departure is also unrecorded, but the WLB was sold to John Ivor Jones of Silver Star in May 1937, raising the possibility of further unknown rolling stock. It could be that the REO survived until June 1946 when the next recorded vehicles arrived in the shape of two Bedfords, a three year old OWB utility bus and a pre-war WTB. A third Bedford, a post-war OB/Duple Vista coach, came from Pye of Colwyn Bay in July 1949. The OB coach remained in service for 16 years but the two older Bedfords were retired in the 1950s, replaced by a pre-war TS8 Tiger/Burlingham bus (new to Ribble but acquired from Clynnog & Trevor in September 1956) and a 1949 Crossley SD42/Burlingham coach which arrived in September 1957. The latter machine (JC 9962) had been new to Ellis Blue Motors of Llanllechid and had passed with that business to Crosville in 1952. Surprisingly, they kept it for five years before selling it on, via a dealer, to Williams.

In August 1959 the TS8 was replaced by a post-war Tiger, a PS1/Roe bus acquired from Yorkshire Traction which would last for more than a decade as the main vehicle on the Pwllheli run. The Crossley coach was sold in April 1962, its place in the fleet taken by a Bedford SBG/Duple Super Vega purchased from James of Liverpool, and in September 1965 a newer version of the same combination came from Purple Motors of Bethesda to replace the OB.

Mr MH Williams had passed away in the early 1960s and his widow, Mrs Eleanor Williams, became the new proprietor. In December 1967 she sold the Liverpool registered SBG to Pioneer of Kenfig Hill in South Wales, replacing it six months later with a Tiger Cub/Duple Britannia coach acquired from another South Wales operator, Jones of Aberbeeg. This machine, WND 477, had been new to Spencer of Manchester and in the mid-1980s would be acquired by Spencer's linear descendant, the Shearings group, as a heritage vehicle. It later returned to North Wales to perform similar duties with Alpine of Llandudno.

By March 1970 the PS1/Roe bus was well past its prime and was replaced by a Bedford C5Z1 with 30-seat bus bodywork by Duple (Midland). OTY 208 had been new to Tait of Morpeth in 1959, passing to Corvedale of Ludlow in March 1962, to Teme Valley of Leintwardine in June 1962, then to Davies Brothers of Pencader in April 1966 and Dengate of Buckley in September 1967. Its journey had taken it from Northumberland to Shropshire, Herefordshire, Carmarthenshire, and Sussex before its arrival on the Lleyn peninsula. As far as can be confirmed the little Bedford was the first vehicle in the Williams fleet to carry the 'Llithfaen Motors' fleetname. It gave another decade of service to Williams and then received its reward by being preserved for posterity by William Hughes – once an employee of the company.

The business passed from Mrs Williams to her son, Gwyn Harris Williams, who guided it through the minefield of deregulation. Later service buses were also Bedfords, but of considerably greater length than OTY 208. A 1970 YRQ with 45-seat Willowbrook dual-purpose bodywork (new to Salopia of Whitchurch but acquired from Morris of Llanfyllin) replaced the C5Z1 in July 1980, and in 2010 was still parked in the Llithfaen area awaiting attention by its new (preservationist) owner. The YRQ's replacement was a 1981

YMQ with a 50-seat Duple Dominant bus body, coincidentally acquired from Davies Brothers who had also had the pleasure of OTY 208's presence for a time in the mid-1960s. Like the C5Z1 and YRQ buses before it, it received the 'red front' livery demanded by Gwynedd County Council for all vehicles used on tendered services.

In the deregulated era the neighbouring business of Nefyn Coaches had become a major provider of such tendered services, starting with the Dinas to Pwllheli routes formerly operated by Caelloi Motors. When Mr GH Williams decided to retire in June 2000 the Llithfaen service, the YMQ, and the (withdrawn) YRQ passed to Nefyn Coaches who quickly became the largest bus operator on the Lleyn peninsula. Crosville had abandoned most of its rural services in the area in the late 1960s and early 1970s, and by the time of Williams' disappearance the Crosville company itself had departed, its remaining Welsh assets consumed by the aquamarine monster known as Arriva. The Llithfaen to Pwllheli route had remained in local hands all the way through from the 1920s, almost as if Crosville had never been there.

PART TWO

DENBIGHSHIRE & FLINTSHIRE

Denbighshire had a narrow coastal strip which included the major resorts of Colwyn Bay and Rhos-on-Sea (with a combined population of more than 25,000), but most of the county was in the mountains and hills to the south and sparsely populated except for an area in the southeast around the mining town of Wrexham. Coal and iron had been extracted from the area around Wrexham since prehistoric times, but the demands of the Industrial Revolution saw the town grow from around 2,000 inhabitants in 1700 to more than 40,000 by 1900. This made it the largest town in all of North Wales. The county town of Denbigh, which saw little growth during the same period, retained a population of between 6,000 and 8,000 but lost most of its medieval status to the newer boom-towns of leisure and coal. Regional centres elsewhere in the county included Llangollen in the Dee valley (famous for the Eisteddfod), and Ruthin.

Flintshire came in two parts, separated by territory belonging to Denbighshire and the English county of Cheshire. The northern part had a coastline on the Irish Sea, the site of important resorts such as Rhyl (which grew from 2,000 inhabitants in 1800 to ten times that number in 1900), Prestatyn, and Abergele. It was also an important coal and iron mining region and later industry included a major steelworks at Shotton, and the development of an aircraft factory at Hawarden, close to the English border. Market towns in this northern section of the county included Flint and Connah's Quay on the Dee estuary and the inland communities of Holywell and Mold. By contrast, the southern part of Flintshire was almost entirely rural and possessed no towns at all, being a landscape of small villages, farmers' fields, and peat bogs. On maps this area was usually referred to as 'Flintshire (Detached)'.

Bryn Melyn of Llangollen

In one (probably apocryphal) story, widely repeated in bus-related publications over the years, Anthony 'Laddie' Jones – the co-founder of Bryn Melyn Motor Services – had made enough money to buy his first bus by carrying goods through the streets of Llangollen on a hand-cart. It may well be true that an adolescent Jones undertook such activity, but his family background was nowhere near as humble as this legend implies. The Jones family were from the village of Rhewl, a few miles to the northwest of Llangollen, where they owned a smallholding called 'Bryn Melyn'. By 1922, the date usually given for the hand-cart story, Richard Noel Jones and Anthony Jones were already the co-proprietors of the Bryn Melyn Motor Company which owned a garage on Abbey Road in Llangollen, offering petrol, new and second-hand cars, driving tuition, and car-hire. Anthony lived in a three storey house adjacent to the garage known as 'Dolhiryd'.

In 1923 the company started a regular service from Rhewl to Llangollen on Tuesdays, Fridays, and Saturdays, initially operated by hire-cars from the garage rather than by buses. A second service

Williams of Llithfaen bought this PS1 Tiger/Roe bus, AHE 784, from Yorkshire Traction in August 1959 and repainted it in their chocolate brown and cream livery. The lettering behind the entrance door reads 'Please pay as you enter', possibly indicating that some kind of modification has taken place to facilitate this course of action. The Tiger was replaced by a Bedford C5Z1/Duple (Midland) 30-seat bus in March 1970. *(Peter Yeomans)*

Petrol-engined Bedford SB3/Duple Super Vega coach HCC 850 was new to Purple Motors of Bethesda in 1960, and was sold to Williams of Llithfaen in September 1965. It replaced a 16 year old Bedford OB/Duple Vista. *(Author's Collection)*

Bryn Melyn Motor Services suffered from a severe shortage of capacity during the Second World War and requested an allocation of utility vehicles to help relieve its overloaded fleet. The Ministry approved the purchase of a double-decker in early 1945, but the vehicle – a Bristol K6A with Strachan lowbridge bodywork registered DCA 371 – was delayed by timber shortages and finally arrived at Llangollen in January 1946. Here it is at the depot in the late 1950s. The vehicle was withdrawn and scrapped in July 1959. *(AD Broughall via Peter Harden)*

Dennis Lancet J3/Yeates coach ENT 926 was originally ordered by Hampson of Oswestry (hence the Shropshire registration) and delivered to them in June 1948. Within a few months it had been resold to Bryn Melyn who kept it for more than a decade, selling it to Central of Newton Aycliffe in February 1959. *(Peter Harden Collection)*

from the village of Pentredewr to Llangollen soon followed, operating on the same days of the week, and both routes used a town terminus on Berwyn Street, across the road from the Armoury. The services proved to be popular and in February 1924 the first bus arrived, an 18-seat Graham registered CA 6432 which avoided the need for expensive duplication on the busiest shopping days.

According to one report this vehicle was kept, from new, at premises on Berwyn Street (which is to the south of the Rover Dee, while the known garage was on Abbey Road which is across the historic bridge on the northern side) but this may be a misunderstanding. However, in March 1927 three members of the family, Richard Noel Jones, Anthony Jones, and Elsie Marjorie Jones, jointly acquired a shop (with living accommodation above it) at 6 Berwyn Street from a Mr Churchill. At around the same time the three Joneses established a new partnership to operate the two bus routes, trading as Bryn Melyn Motor Services from the Berwyn Street address. The partnership's business was described as a mixture of 'motor proprietors, cycle, and music agents', the latter two activities providing the main income from the shop.

A major expansion of the partnership's stage carriage activities took place in 1928 when the Joneses acquired a six days per week route from Chirk to Glyn Ceiriog previously operated by Alfred Wright of Rhosymedre. Wright was the brother of the founder of Wright of Penycae (qv) and had decided to concentrate on his other services to local collieries. Bryn Melyn extended the route to operate from their base in Llangollen, creating a horseshoe-shaped service which ran seven miles eastwards along the Dee valley from Llangollen, three miles southwards through Chirk (where it connected with mainline railway trains), and then seven miles westwards to Glyn Ceiriog. It was to remain their most important service for more than 50 years. Another new service, started in 1929, ran from Llangollen to Oswestry via Chirk on the Shropshire town's market-days (Wednesdays and Saturdays) only, and would provide another valuable source of income over the following seven decades.

All four of Bryn Melyn's routes were approved by the new Traffic Commissioners in 1931, and the schedules attached to the licence applications show that at least three vehicles were required by then, especially on Saturdays. Few of the buses operated before 1943 have been identified. The original Graham had been sold in 1931 and the only other known vehicles from the 1930s were a 14-seat Dodge (UN 3870) acquired from Evans of Wrexham (qv) in 1933 and sold in 1935, and a 26-seat Bedford WTB (AUN 884) delivered in January 1938.

The partnership between the Joneses was dissolved on 29th February 1936, leaving Anthony Jones as the sole proprietor of Bryn Melyn Motor Services. On 21st February 1939 Richard Noel Jones sold the property on Berwyn Street (he was by that time its solitary owner) to Anthony Jones and then moved to Chepstow in Monmouthshire. In April 1939 Anthony Jones took out a second mortgage on 6 Berwyn Street, and in May 1939 the 'London Gazette' carried a somewhat belated announcement of the dissolution of the partnership more than three years previously. I suspect that all of this might make sense to an accountant. It appears that Anthony Jones did move into the Berwyn Street address as work began almost immediately to convert 'Dolhiryd' into offices for the bus company.

The outbreak of war in September 1939 and the petrol rationing which followed reduced the garage's revenues to a drastic extent, but the bus company continued to prosper. While the frequency of the Llangollen to Glyn Ceiriog route was reduced, compensation came from government contracts to operate journeys to local coalmines and other strategic workplaces. Several second-hand vehicles (including two more WTBs) were added to the fleet in 1940/1 for this purpose but all remain unidentifiable as the old photographs which reveal their existence do not show more than 'partial' registration marks. The next two deliveries, a brace of Bedford OWB utility buses which arrived in February 1943, marked the point at which Bryn Melyn's known fleet history truly began. A third OWB was delivered in late 1944.

A fourth utility vehicle, a Bristol K6A with Strachan lowbridge bodywork, was actually delivered just after the end of the war. It was Bryn Melyn's first double-decker and found peacetime employment on the Glyn Ceiriog and Oswestry services. Business was booming and more revenue came from the reopened filling station and associated motor-car activities. To celebrate his increasing prosperity Anthony Jones bought a run-down manor house at Eglwyseg, in the hills to the north of Llangollen, in 1946. After a full restoration it became his new home in the following year, and the surrounding farmland was used to establish a herd of Welsh Black cattle. In July 1947 he made another important move when Bryn Melyn Motor Services became a limited company.

In the immediate post-war era there was a surge in demand for coach outings and Jones decided to have his share of the business. In August 1948 a virtually brand-new 33-seat Dennis Lancet J3/Yeates coach was acquired from Hampson of Oswestry, and a similar machine but with bodywork by Santus arrived fresh from the coachbuilder's factory in Wigan in July 1949. A third new coach, but this time a 35-seat Bristol L6A/Yeates, was delivered in time for the 1950 summer season. It was one of the last new Bristol vehicles to reach an independent operator before the manufacturer's output became restricted to state-owned customers.

The newest of the three OWBs had gone first, sold to Jones of Market Drayton in March 1946. One of the preceding pair went to Mid-Wales Motorways in May 1951. No replacements are recorded (it could be that the new coaches covered their former duties), but in early 1954 Bryn Melyn received its second double-decker. Like the Bristol K6A it had an AEC engine, but this time mounted on an AEC Regent chassis delivered to London Transport in 1935 as fleet-number STL 1033. The bodywork of BLH 897 was also very different, as the vehicle had been fitted with a forward entrance for use on 'Country Area' services. The other delivery in 1954 was at the opposite end of the capacity range, being a 7-seat Trojan.

The following year's arrivals were equally worthy of comment. MHN 601/2 were Morris-Beadle integrals with rear entrance 35-seat bus bodywork. New to United Automobile Services in 1950, they failed to impress and came to Bryn Melyn via Lancashire Motor Traders in August 1955, replacing the final OWB and allowing the coaches to be available on weekdays for private-hire work. United had found the vehicles to be rather under-powered, but most of Bryn Melyn's mileage was 'down in the valleys' rather than 'over the hills' so their poor performance could be tolerated given the bargain purchase price.

The front entrance STL came to the end of its natural life in 1957 and the machine was replaced by a heavily rebuilt Daimler CWA6 utility bus. New to Midland Red, GHA 946 had received an odd-looking 'built up' nearside front wing and various other BMMO refinements to make it even uglier than the average utility double-decker. Bryn Melyn bought it from its second owner, Lloyd of Oswestry. The same year brought yet another unusual creature to Llangollen, a 43-seat Daimler Freeline/Metalcraft coach which had started life with the Don Everall fleet in Wolverhampton but came to Bryn Melyn from Black & White of Bilston. It replaced the 1949 Lancet J3/Santus coach. In 1959 the other Lancet was replaced by another second-hand Freeline (this time with Heaver bodywork), the Morris-Beadles by two BBW-bodied saloons from Red & White (one a PS1 Tiger, the other an Albion Valkyrie), and the two utility double-deckers by a single post-war AEC Regent III acquired from Rhondda.

The Regent III was the fourth AEC powered double-decker to serve in the Bryn Melyn fleet and also the last. After just a year in Llangollen it was sold and replaced by no fewer than three Bristol K5Gs with lowbridge Willowbrook bodies (and Gardner engines) which came from North Western in August 1960. Their duties included the Glyn Ceiriog route, occasional visits to Oswestry on market-days, and a new works service to a Wrexham area colliery. At the lighter end of the fleet the 7-seat Trojan was joined by a nine year old 14-seat Karrier in October 1961. The next arrival, a 41-seat Albion Aberdonian/Plaxton coach which was acquired third-hand in March 1962, fell between the two extremes.

One of the K5G double-deckers was withdrawn in August 1962, and another in 1963 after the loss of the works contract, leaving one survivor to maintain the trunk route to Glyn Ceiriog. It would continue to do so for a while under Bryn Melyn's new proprietor. In 1964 Anthony Jones decided to retire (to spend more time with his cows?) and sold the company to Alfred 'Ted' Broadhurst.

Broadhurst was a larger than life character. Born in Lewisham in south London in 1919, he was the son of a successful motor trader. In 1941 his father, sick of the Luftwaffe's bombing raids, decided to close up the family's London house and to move to Llangollen in the comparatively peaceful Dee valley. He bought a local garage

Anthony 'Laddie' Jones, the proprietor of Bryn Melyn, was impressed enough by the K6A's combination of Bristol chassis and an AEC engine to order a single-decker coach with the same running units just before the legislation which restricted Bristol and ECW products to state-owned customers. The vehicle eventually materialised in 1950 as a 35-seat Yeates-bodied L6A registered GCA 767 and was one of the last Bristols delivered to a private sector operator until the late 1960s. Here it is seen outside the Dorothy Cinema in Llangollen, suffering from that location's habitual tree shadow. *(AD Broughall via Peter Harden)*

Bryn Melyn's growing reputation as an 'interesting' fleet was further enhanced in early 1954 by the arrival of this STL class AEC Regent, BLH 897, from London Transport. New in 1935 as STL1033 it carried a 52-seat forward entrance body designed for use on Country Area services. It served in Llangollen until 1957 when it was replaced by a Daimler CWA6 utility bus acquired from Lloyd of Oswestry but new to Midland Red. *(G Mead via Peter Harden)*

This 7-seat Trojan M56, basically a van with windows, was new to Bryn Melyn in July 1954 and was used on the village services and on private-hire work. KUN 524 lasted for a highly creditable 11 years before being scrapped in the summer of 1965. *(Peter Harden Collection)*

In 1950 the Tilling group company United Automobile Services acquired a pair of 35-seat Morris-Beadle buses registered MHN 601/2. Delivered as fleet numbers CBM 1/2, they became M1/2 in May 1951. Both were sold to Bryn Melyn in August 1955 but proved to be mechanically troublesome and had gone by the end of 1959. MHN 601 is seen outside the Dorothy Cinema, with the offending tree in shot for a change. The destination blind reads 'Rhewl & Llangollen 2' providing rare evidence that Bryn Melyn did use route numbers. *(Richard Winter)*

The former Hampson Lancet J3 was replaced by this unique Daimler Freeline with a 41-seat coach body by Heaver of Durrington. KWP 27 came to Bryn Melyn from Supreme of Stourbridge in 1959 and was sold to the Don Everall dealership in early 1962. In this shot it is awaiting departure outside the Dorothy Cinema. *(AD Broughall via Peter Harden)*

The two Morris-Beadles were replaced by a pair of 35-seat BBW-bodied buses acquired from Red & White. One was a PS1 Tiger, the other this Albion Valkyrie EWO 768. Formerly Red & White's fleet number S2547, it arrived in Llangollen in August 1959 and gave just over three years of service to its new operator. The sun is shining brightly on the Dorothy Cinema, making the tree across the road even more annoying than usual. *(Peter Harden Collection)*

In August 1960 Bryn Melyn bought three Bristol K5G double-deckers from the North Western Road Car Co. They were pre-war machines which had been rebodied by Willowbrook in the early 1950s. AJA 160 (previously NWRCC's fleet number 440) was the longest lived of the trio, staying with Bryn Melyn until March 1965. Here it is seen in Glyn Ceiriog, close to the 'Motories' premises of local operator LG Phillips. Visible in the background are Phillips' Commer recovery vehicle and Bedford OB/Duple coach CNL 312. The latter was sold in August 1961, narrowing the date of this image down to a single 12 month period. *(AM Davies via Anthony Moyes)*

Bryn Melyn acquired a trio of brand-new Bedford SB5 buses with 42-seat Willowbrook bodywork in the early 1970s. This is the last of the three, CCA 768L, delivered in 1973. It was the only one of the machines to survive deregulation and to be painted in Bryn Melyn's 1980s livery of a red roof, yellow window surrounds, and blue lower panels. *(JT Williams Collection)*

and motor-spares company, Davies Brothers, to keep himself busy and (inevitably) came into regular contact with Anthony 'Laddie' Jones. In 1958 Broadhurst senior died and his son left his job in the London area to run the family business in Llangollen. His first move was to rename it. 'Davies Brothers of Llangollen' became 'Deeside Broadhurst Ltd' which meant that the company's recovery vehicles and delivery vans could retain their 'DBL' corporate logos.

'Ted' Broadhurst had three existing hobbies; collecting vintage cars, sailing (he had a 50ft ocean-going yacht) and model railways. In 1964 Bryn Melyn Motor Services became his fourth hobby. To help pay for the purchase he decided to sell off Bryn Melyn's coaching business, including excursion and tour licences from the Llangollen area. This was facilitated by establishing a new subsidiary, Deeside Garage Ltd, to hold the relevant licences and by modernising the rolling stock. A one year old Bedford SB5/Duple Bella Vega coach joined the Albion Aberdonian, replacing an ageing Bedford SB/Burlingham coach which was transferred to the bus company. The Trojan and the Karrier were also withdrawn and replaced by a single brand-new Bedford CALZ30/Martin Walter 11-seat minicoach. With the modernisation completed the Deeside Garage business was sold to the Roberts brothers of Cefn Mawr in December 1965. The brothers' father and uncle had operated in the Cefn Mawr area as Roberts' Coaches for many years. The deal with Broadhurst did not include the Deeside Garage name and the Roberts siblings created their own new company, Vale of Llangollen Travel Ltd, to assume control of the acquired assets.

Broadhurst was also reshaping the bus fleet. The two half-cab saloons acquired from Red & White were withdrawn in 1964, replaced by a Bedford SB1/Duple (Midland) service bus acquired from Williams of Ponciau (qv) and two elderly SB/Burlingham coaches, one of them (as mentioned above) repatriated from Deeside Garage. The final K5G double-decker was withdrawn in March 1965 as declining passenger loads on the Glyn Ceiriog service no longer justified its increasingly expensive maintenance, while two 11-seat Morris J2 minibuses were acquired for the market-day services from Rhewl and Pentredwr to Llangollen, liberating a larger vehicle to replace the K5G on the trunk route.

The two SB/Burlingham coaches were replaced in 1966/7 by two more SB/Duple (Midland) buses, both of them second-hand. The combination became the mainstay of the fleet during the Broadhurst era and all three existing machines were replaced by brand-new versions of the same basic design (by then badged as Willowbrook-bodied products) in 1971/3. In the mid-1970s the minibus fleet was also updated, the Morris J2s being replaced by two Ford Transits.

In 1980 Broadhurst established the Llangollen Motor Museum to display his collection of vintage cars to the public. His next major expenditure was on Bryn Melyn's first double-decker in 17 years, an Alexander-bodied Fleetline which came from Midland Scottish in July 1982. Bought for use on a lucrative schools contract, it was 'Ted' Broadhurst's final gift to the company. Rapidly approaching his 65th birthday he had decided to retire from business and to concentrate on the Motor Museum, his yacht, and his model railway layouts. In 1983 he let it be known that Bryn Melyn would soon be for sale and found a ready buyer amongst his own staff at Deeside Broadhurst.

Terry Bluck had worked for Broadhurst for 30 years, latterly as the manager of the Bryn Melyn subsidiary. He knew the company better than anyone but Broadhurst himself and was convinced that he could make it pay its way as an independent entity. He secured the endorsement of another Deeside Broadhurst employee, Clive Wilson, and together they bought Bryn Melyn Motor Services in September 1983, allowing 'Ted' Broadhurst to retire a little earlier than he had anticipated.

As one might expect, the new owners had their own ideas of how to improve the business. The first noticeable change came almost immediately when a Ford R192/Willowbrook service bus, acquired from Williams of Ponciau, replaced the oldest of the SB buses. Relaxation of licensing regulations (under the 1980 Act) allowed Bryn Melyn a successful application to increase the Oswestry service to six days each week rather than the previous two. The traditional Bryn Melyn livery of 'Asian Blue' and cream was also modernised by the addition of red roofs and yellow window surrounds. It was garish, and not to everybody's taste, but it was distinctive.

Further changes took place after deregulation

in October 1986. The Fleetline was withdrawn in early 1987 and not immediately replaced, although a Ford R1114/Van Hool coach acquired in the same year maintained the fleet strength, while in 1988 the two rather spartan Transit minibuses gave way to two new Mercedes-Benz units with 25-seat dual-purpose bodywork by PMT. In 1989 the pace of change quickened markedly when Bryn Melyn introduced a new 'X5' shuttle service between Llangollen and Wrexham, operating every 15 minutes on Monday to Saturday daytimes. Meanwhile, the Glyn Ceiriog service had become route 64 and the augmented service to Oswestry the 419, giving the impression of a much larger company.

The next decade would see a huge expansion of the Bryn Melyn fleet, mainly due to the outstanding popularity of the X5. Double-deckers returned to the fleet with the acquisition of three Bristol VRT3/ECW vehicles in 1996-8, followed by two East Lancs-bodied Dennis Dominators. The first of these came from London & Country in 1998, the other from North Western in 2001, reviving old memories of the STL and the K5Gs which had come from operators with similar names to these post-deregulation entities. There were also many second and third hand examples of a wide variety of single-decker types including a Leyland Lynx from Brighton & Hove and two MAN/Optare Vectras from Chambers of Bures.

The company would later be acquired by the GHA group, but would be maintained as a distinct operating unit, known as Bryn Melyn Ltd and based at new premises in Ruabon – more or less the mid-point of the X5. Few could have foreseen that this (traditionally) rather eccentric operator would become one of the resounding commercial success stories of the deregulated era. It could never have happened without the pioneering groundwork of Anthony 'Laddie' Jones, the community spirit (and charitable nature) of Alfred 'Ted' Broadhurst, or the business instincts of Terry Bluck. The present-day Bryn Melyn is a tribute to them all.

Chaloner of Moss

Timothy Chaloner operated a taxi service between the suburban village of Moss and Wrexham town centre in the mid-1920s. In 1929 he bought a 20-seat Dennis bus from Phillips of Holywell (qv)

and became a timetabled bus operator, employing his younger brother Samuel as his conductor. Local people in Moss liked the Chaloner brothers and their business was profitable from the start, despite competitive pressure from much larger operators.

The original Dennis was replaced by a third-hand Thornycroft A2 in 1935, but this proved to be unreliable and in December 1936 it was traded in as part-payment for a four year old 32-seat Dennis Lancet. In one famous story, repeated through several generations, Mr Chaloner had some difficulties with manoeuvring this much larger vehicle into its overnight parking space. On one occasion, allegedly after enjoying a pint at the end of his driving day, he reversed the Lancet into a gas pipe on the side of a building. Amazingly, no explosion ensued but the village of Moss was without a mains gas supply until the broken pipe could be repaired. Tim Chaloner was inclined to remain as a one bus operator, but wartime demand led to the arrival of a second vehicle in June 1943. This was a 26-seat Bedford WTB which came from a Shropshire operator but had been new in 1936 to Parker (Blue Bird) of Oldham.

The founder died in 1946, when only 46 years old. His widow Doris took control of the company, employing a driver and continuing as the conductress on the service to Moss (she had replaced Samuel Chaloner on these duties in the mid-1930s). Tim and Doris's son, Edward Chaloner, later joined his mother in the business which then traded as D Chaloner & Son. A strange purchase in July 1946, taking the fleet to three vehicles, was a 20-seat 1931 vintage Dennis GL - almost identical to Tim Chaloner's very first bus. It could well be that this vehicle was purchased as a tribute to the departed founder, but this has proven impossible to confirm. It was sold in November 1949 at the end of a year in which the whole fleet had changed. The WTB had gone in January, replaced by a brand-new Bedford OB/Duple Vista coach – Chaloner's first ever new vehicle. In September the Lancet had also departed, its place on the Moss route taken by a third-hand Bedford OWB acquired from Mid-Wales Motorways. The small Dennis was not replaced, cutting the 'fleet back to two vehicles.

In November 1953 the OWB was sold to Llynfi Motors in South Wales. Its replacement, HB 6592 (ironically a post-war Dennis Lancet) had a 33-

GUE 249 was another of the Stratford Blue PS1 Tiger/NCB buses, and found its way to the Wrexham area via its second owner, the Porthcawl Omnibus Co. Chaloner of Moss bought it from them in October 1960 and it is seen here leaving King Street bus station for the operator's home village. *(Roy Marshall via Lawrence Corrieri)*

This 1954 Bedford SBG received its 40-seat bus bodywork in the Kegworth premises which Duple acquired from Nudd Bros & Lockyer, but before the establishment of the separate Duple (Midland) subsidiary. As a result its bodywork is accurately described as plain old 'Duple'. New to Johnson of Southsea it passed to Chaloner in February 1962 and is seen on the Moss route in King Street bus station. *(Peter Harden Collection)*

Davies Bros of Summerhill bought this Crossley Mancunian with 52-seat English Electric bodywork from a dealer in March 1950. It had been new to Ashton-under-Lyne Corporation in 1935 as fleet number nine. Seen here in the bus station in Wrexham, the Crosville vehicles visible in the background include an all-Leyland PD2 on its way to Llay and GCD 684, a Park Royal-bodied TD7 diverted from Southdown, en route to Bradley. *(DJ Stanier)*

If the Davies Bros fleet had been locked away in a secure building at the time of the company's closure (rather than sent to the scrapyard) it would now be worth a fortune. Among the prize specimens in use at the end was this pre-war Dennis Lancet with a 32-seat Dennis coach body, TJ 9083, which had arrived from Mercer of Longridge in May 1951. *(DJ Stanier)*

seat coach body built by its first operator, Davies of Merthyr Tydfil. The 1949 OB coach left the fleet in April 1956, replaced by an older vehicle with a younger body. This was BCF 284, a pre-war AEC Regal rejuvenated by the addition of a new, fully-fronted Duple coach body in 1953. This work had been undertaken to the order of its previous operator, Morley of West Row in Suffolk.

The Regal and the post-war Lancet were both withdrawn from use in November 1960. Their solitary replacement was a PS1 Tiger/Northern Coach Builders bus, GUE 249, which had been new to Stratford Blue but came to the Wrexham area from Porthcawl Omnibus in South Wales. Another vehicle from the same batch operated alongside it in Wrexham on behalf of Phillips of Rhostyllen (qv) while two of its other siblings served in North Wales with Deiniolen Motors and Purple of Bethesda. Chaloner of Moss had become a one horse operator again as its founder had envisaged. By this time Edward Chaloner was doing most of the driving, with his sister Iris serving as the conductress, and their mother taking care of administrative matters.

The Tiger's reign was brief. In February 1962 the Chaloners replaced it with an eight year old Bedford SBG/Duple bus, LCA 591, acquired from their near neighbours Johnson of Southsea (qv). The Johnson family had decided to sell out to Crosville. The SBG had reached its 22nd year by the time of its own retirement in April 1976. Impressed by the vehicle's economical performance (especially for a petrol-powered machine) and unexpected longevity, the Chaloners decided to replace it with a new one. This materialised as LCA 331P, a diesel-engined SB5 with a body badged as a Willowbrook product although the design had changed very little since LCA 591's creation back in 1954. The new Bedford would also be a long-lived and faithful servant to the family, surviving until 1991 when it was replaced by a Mercedes-Benz 811D with 33-seat Reeve Burgess bodywork. Doris Chaloner had only experienced the first two years of the SB5's long career as she passed away in 1978, 32 years after her husband.

Despite the small scale of the Chaloner enterprise it continued to be profitable after deregulation and, like Bryn Melyn, was eventually acquired by the booming GHA group. For more

than 70 years the Chaloner family had proven that a 'micro operator' could, if well-managed and focused upon a single objective, produce a satisfactory income and survive whether faced by 'The Combine', the Tilling group, the National Bus Company, or the legions of post-deregulation competitors. It was all about passenger loyalty and keeping costs to a bare minimum. Chaloner excelled in both respects.

Davies Brothers of Summerhill

In the 1890s Henry Davies and his wife Ellen established a stables offering horse-drawn conveyances for both goods and passengers. They soon expanded their customer base to include the recently deceased, buying several hearses for funeral work. In the years immediately before and after the First World War the firm gradually shifted its emphasis to motorised vehicles, including a number of passenger carrying wagonettes, and in 1919 the company began timetabled motor-bus services from Summerhill and Moss to Wrexham. Details of the firm's earliest buses remain unrecorded apart from a Lancia which arrived in 1921 and was fitted with a char-a-banc body by Ellis Coachbuilders of Wrexham.

Henry Davies died in 1922 and control of the business then passed to his widow and their three sons, William, Herbert, and Thomas. A second route, a long and infrequent run northwards from Wrexham to Penyfford and Buckley mainly designed for use by workers at various coalmines and other industrial establishments, was introduced under the brothers' management and the fleet of buses steadily grew to reflect this increase in commitments. A brand-new 14-seat Dennis was acquired in 1928, followed by new examples of the Dennis Lancet in 1932 and Albion PH115 in 1936. Second-hand purchases were also made in the 1930s including a 20-seat REO, two 18-seat Dennis Gs, and a 20-seat Dennis Dart.

The Second World War brought a great increase in demand for works services in the Wrexham area, and Davies Brothers (in common with several other local companies) received a large number of government-requisitioned vehicles to cope with this traffic. Among the new arrivals were an LT1 Lion coach from Ribble, a bus-bodied Lion from PMT, two TS series Tigers, two additional Lancets, a Maudslay, a Bedford WTB, and Davies Brothers' first two double-deckers, a Leyland Titan and an Albion Venturer – both from the Glasgow Corporation fleet. A third double-decker, this one a Titan from Yorkshire Traction, followed along with three brand-new Bedford OWB utility buses.

By the end of the war the Davies Brothers fleet had grown from six vehicles to 20. To maintain the business at its new, larger, size, the brothers were aggressive in tendering for post-war works contracts. These were usually awarded to the lowest bidder, so no more new vehicles were acquired, the fleet being repopulated by buses only marginally younger than the old-timers being replaced. The list of post-war arrivals included four Crossley Mancunian double-deckers from Ashton-under-Lyne, four TD5/TD7 Titan double-deckers from Bolton, two Dennis Lancets from West Yorkshire, and three pre-war buses rebodied as coaches. One was an LT5 Lion, new to Devon General in 1933 as a 31-seat bus but rebodied as a coach by Harrington in 1947 to the order of its second owner, Valliant of Ealing. The other two rebodies were TD4c Titans which had started life with Leigh Corporation as lowbridge double-deckers but had also received Harrington coach bodies in the late 1940s. The only other coach acquired in this final period of the company's existence was a pre-war all-Dennis Lancet.

The business entered the 1950s with a fleet of 16 vehicles and an apparently healthy amount of work to keep them occupied, but problems were lurking just below the surface. In 1951 the National Coal Board reduced its subsidy for coalminers' bus services resulting in a 25-50% increase in fares for its employees. Unsurprisingly, many decided to use their bicycles instead and revenues from colliery bus services plummeted despite the increase in fares. More than half of Davies Brothers' revenues came from colliery works services. Very little money was being made and little (if anything) put to one side for fleet replacement.

Faced with the prospect of a massive investment in newer equipment at a time of declining income the Davies family decided to sell the company to Crosville, who were willing to pay a handsome price for the stage carriage services and also saw an advantage in removing a competitor from the local works service arena. The take-over took place on 20th February 1953. Predictably, no vehicles were involved, and most of the Davies Brothers fleet ended up in scrap-yards around the Wrexham area. A few vehicles escaped to give further service to travelling showmen. There were no preservationists in 1953.

Edwards of Bwlchgwyn

George Edwards worked as a driver for a bakery and then for a taxi firm in Coedpoeth before starting his own bus company in 1923. His first vehicle, a 14-seat Ford Model T, was acquired to operate a timetabled route (on Mondays, Thursdays, and Saturdays) from the villages of Llanarmon-yn-Lal and Bwlchgwyn to Wrexham. A second Ford arrived in 1928 and new routes were started from Coedpoeth and Bwlchgwyn to Mold (on Wednesdays for the market) and to Ruthin (on the first Thursday in each month for the livestock auctions). These services, plus excursions from Bwlchgwyn, were all licensed by the new Traffic Commissioners in 1931.

In the same year a new 20-seat Morris was acquired, but all subsequent buses and coaches for more than 50 years would be built on Bedford chassis. These included a 20-seat WLB in 1934 and a 26-seat WTB in 1937 (both new), and a second WTB with rare Tooth of Wrexham bodywork acquired from Owen Brothers of Rhostyllen in July 1948. Post-war Bedfords included three OBs (one a Mulliner-bodied bus the other two Duple-bodied coaches) acquired in 1948-50, and a succession of Bedford SB coaches with bodywork by Duple or Plaxton.

By the early 1950s the founder's health was beginning to restrict his contribution to the business and his son, George Frederick ('Fred') Edwards, gave up his apprenticeship with motor dealer Vincent Greenhous to help run the family firm. In recognition of this sacrifice the company became George Edwards & Son as soon as the younger man reached his 21st birthday. The bus-bodied OB was sold to Hampson of Oswestry in May 1960, and for the next ten years the fleet would consist of just two SB coaches at any given time, although four were owned in total. The services to Mold and Ruthin had been abandoned by then, leaving the three days per week route to Wrexham as the only stage carriage route.

One might suspect that this disdain for further expansion came from the founder, for after his

From 1953 onwards Edwards of Bwlchgwyn abandoned its own brown and cream colour scheme and left second-hand vehicles in the liveries of their previous operators. Bedford SB/Duple Vega coach FFV 34 arrived from Jackson of Blackpool in March 1953, when less than a year old, and retained Jackson's livery of red and cream. It is seen on stand five in Wrexham bus station bound for its home village on a short working of the Llanarmon-yn-Lal route. *(DJ Stanier)*

The next second-hand SB variant came from West (Reliance) of Kelsall and thus carried a red, maroon, and cream livery. By a happy coincidence so did this machine which came from Barfoot Bros (Princess Coaches) of Southampton in 1971 and replaced the Jackson vehicle. 103 GAA had been new to Barfoot in January 1963 and was an SB5 with Plaxton Embassy II bodywork. After retirement by Edwards it entered preservation (with Princess titles) but was recently reported in poor condition at a location in Hampshire. *(DJ Stanier)*

Bedford OWB/Duple utility bus BUX 608 was new to Whittle of Highley but came to Evans of Wrexham from its second owner, Mid-Wales Motorways, in September 1948. Seen in Wrexham's King Street bus station awaiting departure to Acton, it was last reported in use as a storage unit with Hollis of Queensferry in 1966 and was later scrapped. *(TG Turner)*

Evans also received some new Bedfords in the immediate post-war period. Mulliner-bodied OB bus FUN 394 was new in April 1949 and is pictured on stand three in the bus station while on the Rhosnessney route. It was withdrawn from use in May 1964. *(Peter Harden Collection)*

death in the early 1980s the business began to grow. At the time of deregulation in 1986 'Fred' Edwards and his son Gareth were the partners in an enterprise which owned four Bedford coaches of YRQ, YRT, and YMT variants. The service from Llanarmon-yn-Lal and Bwlchgwyn to Wrexham continued after deregulation along with an important new route from Wrexham to Minera. Several full-size buses were acquired for the local services, including a Bedford with Duple Dominant bodywork (new to Maidstone Borough), an Optare Delta, and three Optare Excels, as modern coaches were less suitable for this work than the earlier Bedfords had been. In 2008 the Edwards decided to concentrate on their coaching activities and sold the Wrexham area routes to E Jones & Son of Rhosllanerchrugog. David Jones and his family had first entered the local stage carriage market in 1985 by purchasing the business of Evans of Wrexham (qv).

Evans of Wrexham

Robert Daniel Evans was born in the village of Bwlchgwyn near Wrexham, but in 1902 emigrated to Canada to seek his fortune. He progressed from general labouring to tree-felling to mining, and by 1914 had become the manager of a taxi and trucking business. He then felt prosperous enough to summon his adolescent sweetheart, Martha Ann Jones, to leave her home country and to join him in Canada as his wife. And there the story might have ended before it started (from our viewpoint), but Martha Ann Evans became increasingly homesick – especially after the birth of the couple's son, Clifford Arthur Evans, in 1918. In 1919 her husband agreed that the family should return to Wrexham for an extended visit, partly to assuage his wife's homesickness, and partly so that both of them could see their ageing parents for one last time.

They never returned to Canada, at least not as residents. Robert bought a taxi and put it to work on the busy route between Wrexham and Rhosllanerchrugog. By 1928 the competition on this sector had become particularly fierce and the taxi was transferred to work to the east of Wrexham instead. After reading the 1930 Road Traffic Act Robert Evans realised that the kind of 'shared taxi' services prevalent in the Wrexham area would in future need to be licensed by the

Traffic Commissioners, and that vehicles designed to a much higher standard would be required. He needed a purpose-built bus.

A 14-seat Dodge (UN 3870) was subsequently acquired and in 1931 Robert Evans received a licence for a stage carriage service from Wrexham to Acton and Rhosnessney. The route soon attracted a loyal clientele, and in July 1933 a new 20-seat Dodge replaced its smaller predecessor. The family's triumph was brief. A few weeks after the delivery of the new Dodge the founder died at the age of 49. Martha Ann Evans took over as the new proprietor, and three years later was joined by her 18 year old son who worked as her mechanic and conductor. In due course his contribution was recognised when the company became a partnership known as MA Evans & Son.

The widow and her young son proved to be first-rate entrepreneurs. As traffic increased a second 20-seat Dodge was acquired in 1935. A 26-seat Dodge RBF/Grose coach joined the fleet in December 1936, and a 27-seat Dodge SBF replaced the older of the two Dodge 20-seaters in December 1938. In the summer of 1939 a second 26-seat Dodge RBF coach was delivered (on this occasion with Thurgood bodywork), taking the fleet strength to four vehicles. It was to be a very temporary state of affairs. After the declaration of war in September half of the Evans fleet (the 1935 20-seater and the almost brand-new RBF/Thurgood coach) were requisitioned for allocation elsewhere.

The company struggled on until November 1945 when the two Dodges were returned. Better times were on the way. The government had just opened a women's teacher training college at Cartrefle, close to Rhosnessney, and passenger demand for the stage service soared to an all time high. Additional vehicles were needed and arrived in early 1946 in the shape of two Bedford OWBs acquired from operators in Shropshire. A third example (also from Shropshire) followed in September 1948. Seven vehicles, four pre-war Dodges and three wartime Bedfords, were thus available to transport locals and students alike by the end of 1948.

With revenues sky-rocketing it was time to modernise the fleet. A brand-new 31-seat Bedford OB/Mulliner bus was acquired in April 1949, and a factory fresh 29-seat OB/Duple Vista coach in August 1950. In October 1950 the 1935 vintage

Dodge bus was withdrawn, leaving eight vehicles in the company's inventory. A second OB/Vista coach came from Owen Brothers of Rhostyllen in December 1952, shortly after that business had been taken over by Williams of Ponciau (qv).

Patronage of the stage carriage service gradually began to decline as the route ran through some quite affluent areas where car ownership was becoming more commonplace. During 1953 the 27-seat Dodge bus and the RBF/Grose coach were withdrawn and not replaced, reducing the fleet from nine to seven. The final Dodge, the 1939 Thurgood-bodied coach, would survive until November 1957 when it was replaced by a third OB/Vista acquired from a Lancashire operator. Earlier in the same year one of the three OWB utility buses had been withdrawn as fewer duplicate vehicles needed to be held in reserve.

In January 1959 another of the OWBs died of natural causes and an order was immediately placed for a brand-new 42-seat Bedford SB3/Duple (Midland) bus. It arrived in July and became the primary vehicle on the stage route, supported by the 1949 OB/Mulliner bus and with the surviving OWB as a reserve. No more buses would be acquired, and no more new vehicles of any kind. When the last OWB expired it was not replaced, and when the OB bus fell due for retirement in early 1964 its replacement was a second-hand (and ten year old) Bedford SBG/Duple Super Vega coach. Later in that year the 1950 OB coach gave way to a similar vehicle.

A second stage carriage service licence had been granted in 1962, partially in recognition of the declining traffic on the original route. The new licence allowed some timings from Wrexham to continue past Rhosnessney to Borras Park, except on Sundays. Nevertheless, private-hire work (some of it for Cartrefle college), provided an increasingly large part of the company's total income. The two remaining OB coaches were sold in 1965/6, their places taken by more SB/Super Vegas. The last survivor, GCA 747 (acquired from Owen Brothers in 1952), would become famous in its old age as the first PSV in the fleet of Warstone Motors of Great Wyrley in Staffordshire, a company better known to enthusiasts as the second incarnation of 'Green Bus'.

Clifford Arthur Evans, his wife Olwen, and their two daughters continued to run the business until 1985. By then 67 years old, the founder's son had no great relish for the prospect of deregulation and decided to sell the company. The buyers were Elias Jones & Sons of Rhosllanerchrugog. Elias Jones had acquired a retail coal merchant's round from Wright of Penycae (qv) in the early 1950s. In the late 1960s he had started to operate minibuses as a sideline, and in 1978 acquired three full-size coaches from Phillips of Rhostyllen (qv). Phillips' stage carriage licences had already been sold to Crosville, and the Evans purchase brought the Jones family's first taste of local bus work.

In the deregulated age the Jones companies (the founder's sons split into two different camps) would become important providers of tendered bus services in the Wrexham area, and would later acquire the local bus routes of Edwards of Bwlchgwyn (qv). Little remains to remind the casual observer of the Evans company. Jones retired their last former Evans vehicle (a 1968 SB coach) in 1990. The teacher training college, which gave such an enormous boost to the Rhosnessney route, became a Welsh language high school in the 1980s and most of the traffic to and from this site is now carried by contracted school buses. Perhaps the finest monument to the company is the preserved OB coach, GCA 747, and perhaps - one day – we might see it repainted into the colours of MA Evans & Son of Wrexham.

Fisher of Bronington

There were no significant shopping destinations in the 'detached' part of the county of Flintshire, so when William Fisher established a bus service from the villages in the area in 1920 his vehicles were forced by economic geography to cross the boundary into Shropshire. The initial services ran to Whitchurch, Wem, Ellesmere, and Oswestry on their respective market-days. Fisher had two competitors in his home village of Bronington, Chesworth (trading as Pioneer) and Huntbach. The Chesworths established a major network centred on Whitchurch, with the vast majority of their mileage on routes entirely within Shropshire. Their company would be sold to a Whitchurch based entrepreneur in 1934 and become Salopia Saloon Coaches. Salopia then acquired the Huntbach business, leaving Fisher as the only 'native' stage carriage operator on the Welsh side of the Flintshire/Shropshire border.

By 1928 Fisher's services had also spread northwards into Cheshire, with a Saturday only route from Bronington to Chester and a market-day run from Whitchurch, through Bronington, to the border village of Threapwood. The Denbighshire metropolis of Wrexham would, in theory, have provided Fisher with a closer and more popular destination, but the routes to that town from the southern Flintshire villages had already been claimed by larger entities such as Wrexham & District, Western Transport, and Crosville. Fisher decided at an early point that one should never poke a rhinoceros in the eye.

Few details of Fisher's early fleet appear to have been noted by enthusiasts, and as most were second-hand (and from other parts of Britain) the Flintshire motor taxation records are of little avail. The few which have been identified include LG 1576 (a Daimler CF with a 30-seat bus body), DM 7575 (a 20-seat Thornycroft), CK 4133 (a 32-seat Albion bus), and FM 8585 (a 20-seat Bedford WLB). Acquisitions during the Second World War were all of Bedford manufacture including three second-hand WTBs, two coaches and a bus, and a new OWB utility bus which arrived in 1944. The latter vehicle, equipped with more comfortable seating after the war, would serve the company until 1963. Like most of Fisher's new acquisitions until 1950 it bore a Shropshire registration, reflecting the proximity of the English county to the operator's home base.

A brand-new OB/Duple Vista coach was delivered in 1947, and an identical machine arrived in 1948 along with a Burlingham-bodied Crossley SD42 coach. A third new OB coach, but with Plaxton bodywork, was delivered in 1950. For 1951 the Fisher partnership (by then including the founder's sons William Jr and John Raymond) decided to try a 33-seat Bedford SB/Duple Vega coach, and the SB became the company's new 'standard' vehicle throughout the 1950s and 1960s.

Although a total of 16 stage carriage routes were operated in the post-war era, all of them were market-day or other 'shopping' services and consisted of one or two journeys on one or two days per week. As a result only two vehicles were required to cover the schedules, with coaches available to provide duplicates or maintenance cover. From 1958 onwards the two regular vehicles on the stage services were the wartime OWB (BUX 903) and NKR 529, a Crossley

SD42 with fully-fronted coach bodywork by Brockhouse. This Scottish coachbuilder's products were comparatively scarce to the south of Hadrian's Wall, and this particular vehicle had been new to Mollins Machinery (a manufacturer of tobacco processing equipment) as a staff bus. It was already seven years old at the time of its sale to Fisher but would remain in use until the early 1970s.

As rural car ownership grew (and passenger numbers declined) the company began to concentrate upon its coaching activities, and after the retirement of the OWB in June 1963 no more buses were acquired until after deregulation. This policy continued despite the acquisition of a new stage carriage licence in October 1964. This was for a daily rail replacement service from Whitchurch to Ellesmere and Oswestry, but brought nowhere near as much work in as that statement might suggest. The Traffic Commissioners, in their wisdom, divided the new service between Fisher, Crosville, Hampson of Oswestry, Hyde of Ellesmere, and Salopia of Whitchurch. In July 1966 the Fishers increased their share of this new route by acquiring the business of Hyde of Ellesmere. The deal included two more market-day only services, an ageing SB/Duple Vega coach, a 12-seat Commer minibus, and Hyde's garage which was retained by the new owners. Another part of Hyde's assets was acquired by Hampson of Oswestry, including their OB service bus. A separate partnership, including the founder's grandson William Edward Fisher, was established to run the Ellesmere operation.

Another two market-day services (also in Shropshire) were acquired in January 1974 when M&G Motors of Wem ceased to trade. No more new stage carriage services would be introduced before deregulation, and several of the existing routes would be withdrawn or combined with others after the mid-1970s. Meanwhile, the coaching side of the business continued to grow and by 1980 accounted for more than 90% of the company's revenues. Nevertheless, the family remained committed to their local bus services, now operated by the older coaches in the fleet, and many of the market-day runs continued after deregulation. In addition, the company tendered for an assortment of subsidised work, and in 1987 a 53-seat Leyland Leopard/Alexander Y type bus was acquired from Meredith of Malpas in

Cheshire. It was later joined by several Mercedes-Benz minibuses which maintained most of the market-day and tendered schedules.

In the coaching fleet second-hand Bedfords had remained as the vehicles of choice until 1978 when Ford R1114s became the new favourite, followed by Volvos from 1987 onwards. Both types had been selected by William Edward Fisher who was by then the senior partner. In the year 2000 (at the age of 63) he began to contemplate retirement and, as no family member was willing to take the helm, offered the business for sale. On 30th December 2000 the company was sold to Happy Days of Woodseaves in Staffordshire. The new owners were primarily interested in the Fishers' coaching business (Happy Days had already discontinued most of its own bus routes), and in May 2001 the Fisher subsidiary announced that all of its bus services, with the exception of a few ongoing contracts, would cease at the end of that month. Given the nature of the sparsely populated territory involved, it was something of a miracle that the Fishers had managed to keep them going for so long.

The company is still fondly remembered and has a 'living' tribute to its memory in the shape of the Brockhouse-bodied Crossley NKR 529, which is preserved in Fisher's dark blue and cream livery. Now owned by the Emerton family's 'Bounty Motors' operation, the vehicle has been a regular attendee at bus rallies over the years although currently 'off the road' and enjoying another full refurbishment. When this work is completed it may return to the country lanes of Flintshire as the 'Bounty' collection is based quite nearby in southern Cheshire. To residents of a certain age it will be a very welcome sight and stir many old memories.

Hughes of Llansilin

Llansilin is a medium sized village in the hills to the west of Oswestry, and in 1926 Edward Pryce Hughes began to operate market-day (Wednesday and Saturday) bus services between Llansilin, the neighbouring village of Moelfre, and the Shropshire town. Photographs of his first two vehicles, a 7-seat Ford Model T and an unidentified char-a-banc, can be found in the Introduction to this book.

A third (six days per week) service, from Llansilin to Oswestry via Glacoed and Creiglwyn,

was started in 1934 after lengthy hearings in front of the Traffic Commissioners. Both of the original vehicles had already departed by this time but no record has been found of their immediate replacements. One source mentions a Chevrolet, but the next identifiable purchase was of a 20-seat Bedford WLB from Johnson of Southsea (qv) in February 1936. In November 1939, after war had been declared against Germany, the proprietor was allowed to buy a nine year old Humber car and to license it as a 7-seat PSV. It maintained the market-day service from Moelfre to Oswestry throughout the war on a 'reserved place' basis while the WLB covered the more frequent services from Llansilin.

Additional capacity arrived shortly before the end of the conflict. In May 1945 a seven year old Leyland SKP Cub, with 26-seat coach bodywork by Burlingham, was acquired from Webster of Wigan. The vehicle had been new to Auty's Tours of Bury, hence its registration as EN 7508. In July 1948 the Humber was replaced by an identical (but four years younger) version which was also licensed as a PSV. Two more pre-war Bedford WLB 20-seaters were acquired in 1949/50, taking the 'full-size' fleet strength to four. The two proved to be short-lived, each of them sold after just two years at Llansilin. The WLB acquired from Johnson in 1936 survived until 1953.

The founder had taken his three sons, David, Richard, and John James Hughes, into partnership as they came of age, and after his death in 1950 they continued the business under the 'Hughes Brothers' banner. There was some delay in amending the licences which were not officially transferred to the new (smaller) partnership until 1953.

The fleet went back to four vehicles again in 1952 with the purchase of a 1933 vintage Commer Centaur 20-seater coach and a four year old Bedford OB coach with unusual Trans-United bodywork. The latter vehicle, Hughes Brothers' first OB, came from Bowyer of Northwich. There were no new arrivals in 1953, but in 1954 a 7-seat Bedford shooting-brake was acquired (and licensed as a PSV) along with two more OBs, one a Duple-bodied bus which came from Keeler of Garden Village (qv), the other a fully-fronted Plaxton-bodied coach. A second Plaxton-bodied OB coach was bought from Lloyd of Oswestry in November 1955 and this flurry of newcomers

Owen of Rhostyllen bought this OB/Duple Vista coach, GCA 747, in early 1950. Owen sold out to Williams of Ponciau who declared the OB surplus to requirements and sold it on to Evans in December 1952. The vehicle became better known with a much later operator, Warstone Motors (Green Bus) of Great Wyrley, engaged upon 'heritage' services in southern Staffordshire. *(TG Turner)*

Evans' very last service bus was this petrol-engined Bedford SB3 with Duple (Midland) bodywork, TUN 548, delivered when new in July 1959. It lasted into the early 1970s and after its departure all of Evans' stage carriage services were operated by coaches. *(Peter Harden Collection)*

Photographs of NKR 529 when actually in service with Fisher of Bronington proved impossible to obtain before my deadline for this book. The Crossley SD42 with fully-fronted Brockhouse coach bodywork came to Fisher from its original owners, Mollins Machinery, in 1958 and remained in service until the early 1970s. Now preserved by the Emerton family as part of their 'Bounty Motors' collection, it is seen here at an unidentified bus rally in the 1990s, still wearing Fisher's full blue and cream livery but with an additional 'Emerton' fleetname in the windscreen. *(Author's Collection)*

Hughes Bros of Llansilin replaced their entire fleet in 1958 with a trio of Bedford OB/Duple Vista coaches acquired from Crosville. LFM 404 was the final survivor of the three and was still active on their stage services to Oswestry in 1971. *(Chris Warn Collection)*

allowed the retirement of the SKP Cub and the relatively ancient Commer Centaur. The fleet then stood at four OBs and two 7-seaters.

The Trans-United-bodied OB was sold in April 1957 and the remaining three were withdrawn after the purchase of three OB/Duple Vista coaches previously operated by Crosville in November 1958. They were slightly newer than the Hughes Brothers' existing OBs, had relatively low mileages for their age, and had been well maintained to Tilling group standards by their original owner. As a result one of the trio would remain in service at Llansilin until the early 1970s and the batch repaid its modest purchase price many times over.

While the Llansilin to Oswestry licences had been in the hands of the Hughes family since the 1930s, the licences for a service from the neighbouring village of Rhiwlas to Oswestry had changed hands several times during the same period. In 1956 Thomas Lee of Oswestry sold the Rhiwlas routes to Peter Edwards, also of Oswestry. Edwards used a Pearson-bodied Bedford OB coach, bought from Hampson of Oswestry, on the services. By coincidence, this vehicle had been new to Bowyer of Northwich, and for a few months in 1956/7 could be found in Oswestry at the same time as its former stablemate operating with Hughes Brothers. In June 1959 the brothers acquired the Rhiwlas services from Edwards, but declined his offer to include the OB for a slightly higher price.

In January 1961 the Hughes company acquired its first Bedford SB coach, a 36-seat SBG/Duple Super Vega which had been new to Salopia of Whitchurch in 1954. A second SBG, but with much rarer Thurgood bodywork, arrived in October 1962. This machine, SJH 252, had started its life with Premier of Watford but came to Llansilin from an operator in Wiltshire. It replaced one of the Crosville OBs.

Revenues from the stage carriage services were declining inexorably in the face of a rapid increase in private car ownership, and in April 1966 Hughes Brothers announced a major revision of its local bus services. Seven services were combined into two, with many journeys cancelled and the loss of all departures from a few outlying settlements. Another of the Crosville OBs was withdrawn as a result, leaving just one to operate alongside the two SBGs. The Thurgood-

bodied machine was traded in against a 1961 SB3/ Duple Super Vega in September 1969.

By 1971 the partnership had been reduced to Richard and John James Hughes, and in June 1974 the surviving vehicles and remaining route licences were sold to Mr FG Owen of Corwen in Merionethshire. Fred Owen was virtually unknown at that time, but would become a major player in the region's bus services after moving first to Denbighshire and then to Oswestry – across the border in Shropshire. His interest in the Hughes Brothers routes appeared to be a short-term investment, as in 1977 he sold the services on to Michael Jones, a resident of the Hughes family's home village who adopted the trading name of Llansilin Motor Services. On reflection Fred Owen might have made another, longer-term, investment by selling the services to Michael Jones. At the time of deregulation in October 1986 Llansilin Motor Services was operating one bus (a 45-seat Bedford YRQ with Duple Dominant bodywork), 13 full-size coaches of Bedford, Ford, and Volvo manufacture, and one Ford A/Moseley minicoach. All but two of these 15 vehicles had been acquired from Fred Owen!

Part of the Llansilin business's rapid expansion in the 1980s had been fuelled by Mr Owen's other activities. In early 1982 he had acquired the services of Parish of Morda, including a 'trunk' service from Oswestry to Llanfyllin in Montgomeryshire and the former Gittins brothers' market-day routes to the south of the Shropshire town. A year and a half later, in September 1983, he sold the ex-Parish services to Llansilin Motor Services, using the money to fund a new operation in Oswestry itself – competing on the local routes with Crosville and the reincarnation of the Hampson business. In 1986 Mr Owen's path through the local bus industry swerved again when the Oswestry town services were also sold to Llansilin Motor Services, leaving the great wheeler-dealer free to concentrate upon his expanding coaching empire.

Having, with Mr Owen's help, built up a substantial company from next to nothing, Michael Jones decided to reap the benefits. In 1990 he sold the Oswestry town services to Tanat Valley Coaches, and in 1993 the remainder of the Llansilin business passed to the same purchaser. As a result, Tanat Valley became one of the most important operators of stage carriage services in both southern Denbighshire and in the Oswestry region of Shropshire. Tanat Valley had its roots in Morris of Pentrefelin (qv), a tiny business which had operated a market-day service to Oswestry until 1962. With the acquisition of Michael Jones' assets the company could also claim linear descent from such famous names as Hughes Brothers of Llansilin, Parish of Morda, and Gittins of Crickheath. The local bus industry had come a long way since the days of Edward Pryce Hughes and his momentous decision to buy an 11 year old 7-seat Ford Model T.

Johnson of Southsea

For those unfamiliar with the geography of southern Denbighshire it should be explained that this particular Southsea is a suburb to the west of Wrexham, and by no stretch of the imagination a coastal resort!

Richard Johnson started to offer a pony and trap service from the industrial villages of Talwrn and Southsea to Wrexham town centre in the 1890s. In 1899 he bought a motorised wagonette and by 1916 a 12-seat Ford Model T lorry-bus was in use. The founder's eldest son, Richard Johnson Jr, was also active in the industry by 1924 when he was operating an 18-seat Maudslay char-a-banc under the 'Silver Star' fleet-name.

The Johnsons read the writing on the wall as 'The Combine' assembled itself in 1928/9. To survive in the new environment the family business would need to be consolidated and modernised. The former issue was addressed by the creation of a family partnership known as Richard Johnson & Sons, composed of Richard, Richard Jr, and George and Frank Johnson, the founder's second and third oldest sons. The fleet was modernised by the acquisition of four identical 14-seat Chevrolets, registered to the partnership, to replace the assortment of time-expired PSVs and large taxis previously operated by the individual family members.

The company secured a licence from the new Traffic Commissioners without difficulty, as they could prove that they had been operating a timetabled service over the Talwrn-Wrexham route since 'before the 1914-18 war'. With their source of income thus protected the Johnsons decided to update the fleet in 1931/2. The Chevrolets were traded in against four brand new Bedford WLB buses with 20-seat Waveney bodywork. A fifth was added in 1934 to act as a reserve. In 1936 there was another influx of new vehicles. Out went the WLBs and in came three 26-seat Bedford WTBs and a 32-seat Dennis Lancet, all again brand-new.

In May 1938 another major investment took place when the partnership acquired three new 32-seat Dennis Lancet IIs, with bodywork also by Dennis, registered BCA 234-6. This seemed to indicate that the 1936 machine had performed well as the new Lancets replaced the three remaining Bedfords. The Johnson fleet at the outbreak of the Second World War thus consisted of four Dennis Lancets with an average age of less than two years. As a predictable result of this laudable modernity, the Johnsons received no second-hand or utility bus allocations during the conflict.

In October 1946 the Dennis monopoly was broken when the 1936 Lancet was sold, replaced by a fourth-hand Leyland TS6 Tiger coach of similar vintage. This odd man out was chosen by Maggie, the widow of Richard Johnson Jr who had died prematurely in June 1946. She took his place in the partnership, hiring a driver while continuing to act as the conductress on her share of the timings. Three years later the founder died, his heart undoubtedly broken by the untimely demise of his oldest son. His place in the partnership was taken by a fourth son, Samuel.

Maggie Johnson's pre-war Tiger was sold to Davies Brothers of Summerhill (qv) in February 1950 and replaced by a Bedford OWB acquired from Phillips of Rhostyllen (qv). In May 1950 the first of the 1938 Lancet IIs was sold and its place was taken by a brand-new Thurgood-bodied Lancet J3 coach. The other two 1938 Lancets went in 1954/5, giving way to a pair of 40-seat Bedford SBG/Duple service buses. They were new but rather basic when compared to their coach-seated predecessors. Maggie was still the dissenter when it came to vehicle choice and in February 1956 her OWB was replaced by a two year old Bedford SB3/Duple Super Vega coach acquired from its second owner, the Penmaenmawr Motor Co.

Under the terms of the partnership agreement each partner agreed to select a suitable vehicle (of their own choice if they disagreed with the majority opinion), and to provide a driver and

By all accounts Dennis Lancet J3s were reliable and sturdy vehicles, but they suffered visually from the rather old-fashioned styling of their radiators. Thurgood-bodied coach GCA 664 was new to Johnson of Southsea in May 1950 and is seen here in Wrexham bus station on the operator's stage service to Talwrn. Throughout its life it wore a non-standard livery of white (top) and pale blue (lower) and was an attractive vehicle despite the radiator. Sadly, it was scrapped in January 1962. *(C Carter via Anthony Moyes)*

Johnson's normal colour scheme (using a slightly darker blue on more parts of the bodywork) is shown here on Bedford SBG/Duple bus MUN 91, new in July 1955. After the sale of Johnson's stage service to Crosville this vehicle passed to Hampson of Oswestry in March 1962. *(Peter Harden Collection)*

Most of the Llandudno & Colwyn Bay Electric Railway's tram replacement vehicles were Guy Arab utility buses acquired from Southdown. The L&CBER's fleet number 10 was GUF 388, a Weymann-bodied Arab which had been 488 in the Southdown fleet. Acquired in 1956, it lasted until the end of the tramway company's bus operations in 1961. *(RL Wilson via TG Turner)*

Other vehicles came to the L&CBER from Newcastle Corporation and East Kent. Newcastle's contribution was a pair of pre-war Daimler COG5s which had been converted to open-toppers. The bodywork on HTN 233 (L&CBER fleet number 2) and its sister machine was manufactured by Northern Coach Builders. By August 1960 the pair had been delicensed and they were later scrapped. *(RL Wilson via TG Turner)*

conductor for a set number of hours per week in exchange for an equal share in the surplus revenue. The service required two vehicles, and the hours were split into an early shift and a late shift so that all four partners had a share in each day's work. The shares were rotated from one week to another so that the busiest journeys (the most labour intensive from a conductor's viewpoint) were spread between individual partners. It was a simple system and it worked surprisingly well.

As a mechanism it might have continued to work indefinitely, but by 1961 the four partners were starting to feel their age and were looking forward to retirement. With insufficient interest among the next generation of Johnsons, they had no alternative but to offer the company for sale. Crosville was the obvious buyer and Johnson of Southsea ceased to trade on 22nd October 1961. Crosville had no great wish to add a half-cab Dennis Lancet and three petrol-engined Bedford SBs to its fleet, so the vehicles were retained by the partners and sold off during 1962. One of the SBG buses went to local operator Chaloner of Moss (qv), the other to Hampson of Oswestry, and the SB3/Super Vega to a coach operator in Anglesey. The superb Lancet J3/Thurgood coach had no such luck and ended up in a scrapyard. Its Dennis radiator had made it look slightly old-fashioned even when new, and by 1962 nobody wanted a 12 year old half-cab at any price. Nowadays, of course, preservationists would fight to the death for the right to own such a splendid piece of machinery.

Jones of Llansilin – see Hughes of Llansilin

Jones of Rhosllanerchrugog – see Evans of Wrexham and Phillips of Rhostyllen

Keeler of Garden Village

Garden Village was built in the early 20th century to accommodate an influx of over 3,000 new workers to the expanding Gresford colliery. The development was sited half-way between Wrexham town centre and the colliery to the north. While Wrexham & District (and later Western Transport and then Crosville) provided frequent services along Chester Road, the main artery which ran through the new suburb, the side roads were left to the local independents. As was usual in Wrexham in the 1920s, the services on offer were operated by five to 7-seat taxis and ran on a 'fill and go' basis rather than to a strict timetable. The 1930 Road Traffic Act demanded more formal procedures.

The largest independent on the Garden Village services, FW Strange, progressed to 'full-size' vehicles after obtaining stage carriage licences in 1931, and also maintained a route from Wrexham to the northern suburb of Pandy. The other two Garden Village operators, WT ('Bill') Keeler and George Sugg, stuck with their 7-seaters which were both more manoeuvrable on narrow estate roads and required less maintenance than larger buses. They could also be parked at their owners' homes without attracting hostile comments from neighbours.

In 1946 Bill Keeler decided to take the plunge and buy a full-sized vehicle, trading his 1937 vintage 7-seat Bedford shooting-brake in for a virtually brand-new Bedford OB with 30-seat bus bodywork by Duple. The local people were apparently impressed as demand for Keeler's service rose to fill the new bus, especially after FW Strange sold out to Crosville in March 1947. In the following year George Sugg also gave in to the changing climate and replaced his own 7-seat Bedford with a pre-war 20-seat Bedford WLB.

Keeler doubled his fleet in 1949 by purchasing a brand-new Bedford OB/Duple Vista coach and making an attempt to solicit private-hire work. This venture was impeded by the fact that the Keelers had no telephone, and those wishing to hire the coach were forced to make their enquiry on the service bus or to knock on Bill Keeler's front door. Somehow the OB coach still managed to attract enough work to pay for its hire-purchase instalments.

By 1953 both Bill Keeler and George Sugg had passed their 60th birthdays and jointly decided to retire. Crosville agreed to amend its own services to cover their mileage, and at the end of the year the two small independents ceased to trade.

Llandudno & Colwyn Bay of Rhos-on-Sea

Most of the operators covered in this book started as small family-owned businesses, the only exception so far being the Clynnog & Trevor Motor Co which had a significant number of unrelated shareholders from the very beginning. We now come to the second 'publicly owned' company in this volume, and to one made doubly unusual by the fact that it was an independent tramway operator for almost 50 years before turning to the operation of motor-buses.

The Llandudno & Colwyn Bay Electric Railway Co had a long and tangled history. In 1899 the Light Railway & General Construction Co had sponsored an Act of Parliament authorising the development of a coastal tramway from Colwyn Bay to Deganwy via Rhos-on-Sea and Llandudno. Three years later the company went into liquidation without achieving its goal and was replaced by a new corporate entity, the Llandudno, Colwyn Bay, and Rhyl Electric Traction Co. The word 'Rhyl' was soon dropped from the title as optimism receded, and in 1906 the second company also went into liquidation without operating a single tram.

A third company, the Llandudno & District Electric Construction Co, rose from the ashes and with technical assistance from the NECC group actually managed to build a tramway. The section of track between the depot at Rhos-on-Sea and Llandudno opened for business in October 1907, and that between Rhos-on-Sea and Colwyn Bay in July 1908. In 1909 NECC sold its stake in the company to another major tramway group, Balfour Beatty, and the name of the tramway was changed to the Llandudno & Colwyn Bay Electric Railway. In 1915 the line was extended eastwards from Colwyn Bay to Old Colwyn.

All of the trams were single-deckers (including five second-hand examples bought from Accrington Corporation) until 1936 when ten open-top double-deckers were acquired from Bournemouth. Another two second-hand double-deckers arrived from Darwen Corporation in 1946. With urban tramways closing all over Great Britain it seemed as if there would be no shortage of replacement rolling stock and the future of the company, even if only as a 'Blackpool style' tourist attraction, seemed to be assured.

Things started to go horribly wrong in January 1952 when freak waves destroyed a section of the track at Penrhyn Bay. The damage was eventually repaired but severe storms returned in the following winter and removed another segment of the coastal tramway. The company now found itself unable to insure its assets at any kind of realistic premium, and faced the prospect of financial ruin if any more erosion damage took place. The directors stared into the abyss for a while and then applied to the North West Traffic Commissioners in 1954 for a licence to operate a replacement bus service.

As might have been expected there were many powerful voices raised in objection. The local councils in Colwyn Bay and Llandudno wanted the tramway to continue, as it was a popular feature which brought holidaymakers to the two resorts. On the other hand they were unwilling to offer the company any financial support. Crosville, who held a monopoly of bus services between the two towns, protested even more loudly and tied the new licence application up for more than a year with a series of increasingly more tenuous legal objections. All were dismissed by the Traffic Commissioners who ruled that the L & CBER was entitled to receive a licence as it, in effect, held 'grandfather rights' to the route dating back to 1907/8. The Commissioners did agree to restrict the tramway company's stopping places to an approximation of those previously observed by the trams.

In September 1955 the first double-decker bus arrived at the company's depot in Rhos-on-Sea. AJG 26 was a Park Royal-bodied Leyland TD5 Titan which came from East Kent. Already converted to a driver training vehicle by its previous owner, it continued in this role with L & CBER and was never used in passenger service in North Wales. The first 'real' buses arrived two months later in the shape of two wartime Guy Arab double-deckers acquired from Southdown. Another ten arrived during 1956 (plus one bought for spares) along with two open-top Daimler COG5 double-deckers from Newcastle Corporation. The final tram ran on 24th March 1956.

One of the first two ex-Southdown Arabs was withdrawn from use in August 1957 and replaced by a 13th (active) example from the same batch which was later converted into an open-topper.

Meredith & Jesson of Cefn Mawr bought this 1950 Burlingham-bodied AEC Regal III coach, GDM 223, from Richardson of Buckley (Flintshire) in May 1956. It was a frequent performer on the company's stage service to Wrexham until replaced by a new Plaxton-bodied Bedford SB5 in October 1963. *(David Cunningham)*

AEC Reliance LCA 301 carried a 41-seat Plaxton Venturer coach body and was new to Meredith & Jesson in March 1955. After the closure of the Cefn Mawr operator it passed to nearby coach company Hanmer of Southsea in October 1969 for further service to the people of the Wrexham area. *(Peter Yeomans)*

EG Peters of Llanarmon-yn-Lal treated themselves to a brand-new Foden PVSC6/Burlingham coach in August 1948. FCA 378 is seen in Mold on the market-day service from the operator's home village. It was withdrawn from use in October 1960. *(Roy Marshall via the Omnibus Society)*

Peters took a shine to Commer Avengers, operating several in the late 1950s and the 1960s. The first was Avenger III NUN 450, with Duple 'Super Vega lookalike' bodywork, delivered new in May 1956 and also seen in Mold on the stage service. It was followed by two second-hand Avenger IVs with Duple bodywork, acquired in 1961 and 1965. *(Peter Harden Collection)*

One of the Arabs acquired in 1956 had already received this conversion shortly after its arrival, so for the 1958 summer season the company was operating four open-toppers (two Daimlers and two Arabs) and ten closed-top Arabs. It was probably the company's best year as a bus operator.

Several of the former Southdown Arabs were on their last legs and in January 1959 the two tattiest examples were replaced by two Arabs of a similar vintage acquired from East Kent. A better solution would have been to buy something of more recent origin, but the company was no longer making money having lost its 'unique selling point' with the retirement of the trams. The poor financial state of the company was reflected in the appearance of its vehicles. On several of the Arabs it was possible to read the 'Southdown' fleet-names which had been covered with a single coat of red paint along with that company's apple green livery. The combination of the original green paintwork and the thin red overcoat which disguised their heritage produced a rather odd effect in bright sunlight, where the dark red would fluoresce unevenly like radioactive mud. On most of the vehicles minor damage to panels and other 'non-essential' components of their bodywork was left unrepaired. The fleet looked as scruffy as a scrapyard dog.

By August 1960 the active fleet had declined from 14 vehicles to just six, four of the Southdown Arabs and the two East Kent machines. All of the open-toppers had been delicensed and it was clear that the end was in sight. On 4th April 1961 the directors held an extraordinary general meeting of the company's shareholders, where they announced that Crosville had made an offer of £40,000 for the assets of the L & CBER. Given that the remaining buses were all but worthless it was a surprisingly generous offer, probably motivated by Crosville's fear that a better financed bus operator might move in to seize control of the tramway.

The shareholders took the money and ran before Crosville could change its mind. Services ceased at the end of May and all but one of the vehicles still in use at that time went directly to a breaker's yard. Apart from the peripheral ('Toytown') fleets of the local councils Crosville now held a complete monopoly of bus services in the two largest resorts in North Wales. In a sense nobody was to blame for this state of affairs except for the weather. The directors of the company had the usual duty to ensure the best value for their shareholders, and while another bus operator might well have made a counter-bid to Crosville's offer it seems unlikely that it would have been much in excess of the sum already on the table. There was also an element of uncertainty about the Traffic Commissioners' attitude to such a counter-bid. It is quite possible that a take-over by a party other than Crosville might have resulted in a successful objection to transfer of the 'grandfather rights' enjoyed by the tramway. Sadly we will never know.

Meredith & Jesson of Cefn Mawr

Cefn Mawr is a small town to the south of Wrexham where the traditional employers were the iron mine at Acrefair and the Wynnstay Colliery company. Edward Meredith ran a hardware shop in the town while his son-in-law, James Jesson, operated a horse and cart available for hire as either a goods or passenger conveyance. In 1921 the two men bought a reconditioned (ex US military) Garford lorry and had it converted to carry 24 passengers. The vehicle was acquired to start a scheduled motor-bus service from Cefn Mawr to Wrexham via Ruabon and Johnstown. This operated ten times each day on Mondays, Thursdays, and Saturdays (the local market-days), while on Sundays the Garford made a single round trip to Wrexham Hospital.

Details of other early vehicles have been lost, but in March 1932 the partners acquired a brand-new Commer NF6 with a 32-seat bus body to celebrate the award of licences for their stage carriage services. The Commer proved to be relatively short-lived, as in December 1936 it was traded in against an AEC Regal with a 33-seat coach body manufactured by Watson of Lowestoft. The new vehicle carried details of the four major points on the stage carriage services on illuminated panels above its side windows. Edward Meredith died shortly after the Regal's delivery and his place in the partnership was taken by one of his three sons, Herbert.

The outbreak of war brought additional demand for works services to the local mines and factories, and in May 1940 a two year old Albion

PH115/Duple coach was acquired to cope with this increase in activity. One report suggests that a 32-seat Dennis Lancet was also in use during the conflict, but no confirmation of this has been found.

Herbert Meredith died in 1949 and his share of the business passed to his two brothers, Arthur and George. They were content to allow James Jesson to run the company on their behalf. The next (identified) vehicle arrived long after the end of the war, in September 1951, but was easily worth the wait. HCA 650 was an underfloor-engined AEC Regal IV coach equipped with a stylish 41-seat Bellhouse Hartwell Landmaster body. Despite its luxurious interior it frequently appeared on the stage services to Wrexham alongside the pre-war Regal and Albion half-cabs.

Another new AEC coach, this one a Reliance with a Plaxton Venturer body, arrived in March 1955. It replaced the Albion. In May of the following year the Watson-bodied Regal was also retired, its place in the fleet taken by a second-hand (1950 vintage) Regal III/Burlingham coach acquired from Richardson of Buckley. This survived until October 1963 when it was replaced by a new Bedford SB5/Plaxton Embassy coach.

The fleet remained at three vehicles (the Regal IV, the Reliance, and the SB5) until the summer of 1969 when James Jesson, by then 75 years old, decided to retire. The stage service to Wrexham was sold to Crosville on 16th August but, as was usual in post-war years, the vehicles were of no interest to the purchaser. The Reliance went to local coach operator Hanmer of Southsea, and the SB5 to Mid-Wales Motorways. Sadly, the magnificent Regal IV/Landmaster coach found no buyer and was eventually scrapped. It would have made a fine memorial to this small but fascinating operator.

Morris of Pentrefelin

The small village of Pentrefelin is located in the valley of the River Tanat in the extreme south of Denbighshire, close to the Montgomeryshire border. From 1904 the area was served by the Tanat Valley Light Railway until the passenger service on this line was finally withdrawn in 1951. A supplementary bus service along the valley had been established by the railway while under GWR ownership, and this later passed to Western Transport and then Crosville. The frequency of the bus service from Oswestry gradually increased as rail timings dwindled and then disappeared completely.

William ('Bill') Williams had fought at Gallipoli in the First World War and returned to his home village of Pentrefelin with physical and psychological scars from that infamous bloodbath. On the positive side he had learned to drive during his military service. In 1921 his mother and her second husband, Lewis Morris, helped him to buy a car which he used for private-hire and light goods work around the valley. Four years later he was joined by his younger half-brother, RE (Elvin) Morris and the partnership of Williams & Morris was born.

In the late 1920s a lorry was acquired for use on county council road building contracts, and on Oswestry market-days the vehicle was equipped with seats to carry passengers to the Shropshire metropolis. Demand for these outings was high as many local people considered the railway alternatives (whether by train or by bus) to be too slow and too expensive. Anxious to preserve and develop this new source of income, the half-brothers acquired their first purpose-built bus in 1930, a 19-seat Chevrolet. In the following year Williams & Morris received a licence to legitimise their Wednesday and Saturday trips to Oswestry.

The business expanded in another way in 1931 when a petrol station and garage was opened in Pentrefelin. Over the next few years similar garages would be opened in four neighbouring villages. The partners also acquired a hearse to further diversify their miniature transport empire. In 1933 the Chevrolet was replaced by a 20-seat Bedford WLB as passenger traffic continued to rise.

During the Second World War the Tanat valley became the site of a prisoner-of-war camp and the company received a contract to service the needs of this facility. A 26-seat Bedford WTL coach was acquired from Arthur of Oswestry to cater for this contract which included some long-distance prisoner transfer work. The WLB also made an occasional foray into the wider world, but spent most of the war ferrying prisoners (many of them Italians) from local railway stations to the camp. It also maintained a reduced schedule to Oswestry market.

In late 1949 two second-hand 26-seat WTB coaches arrived and replaced their pre-war Bedford brethren which had both amassed high mileages during the conflict. Shortly afterwards the half-brothers decided to abandon their partnership. Bill Williams took the lorry, the hearse, and the hire-car, along with three of the petrol stations. Elvin Morris received the two coaches and the garage at Pentrefelin. It was an amicable split, made more so to Elvin by the knowledge that the railway line was about to close to passenger traffic. Although this did result in a small increase in numbers on the Oswestry market-day services, all of the additional journeys to replace railway timings went to Crosville.

Despite this unfair allocation of new opportunities business was good enough to allow a modernisation of the 'fleet'. One of the WTBs was sold in December 1952, replaced by a post-war OB/Duple Vista coach acquired from Bowyer of Northwich. Another second-hand OB/Vista coach arrived in September 1956 to replace the other WTB. The company's first diesel-engined coach, a Duple-bodied Commer Avenger IV, replaced one of the OBs in 1961. The other OB was sold in 1962 after the licence for the service to Oswestry was surrendered. A combination of increasing car ownership and competition from the (six days per week) Crosville route had rendered it unprofitable for several years.

And at that point the story should end given the parameters for inclusion in this book, but to finish it there would be unforgivable, for although Elvin Morris remained as a single coach private-hire operator until 1973 greater things were still to come. In 1973 the solitary coach (a petrol-engined Bedford SB3/Duple Super Vega which had replaced the diesel Commer in 1968) was joined by a diesel powered Bedford SB5/Duple (Midland) bus, doubling the size of the fleet. The SB5 had been bought from Bryn Melyn of Llangollen (qv) for use on a schools contract. More expansion came at the end of the decade. In 1979 RE Morris & Sons (as the business had become after Peter and Michael Morris joined their father in a new partnership) acquired Tanat Valley Motors, a petrol station, garage, and Austin-Rover dealership in the larger neighbouring village of Llanrhaeadr-ym-Mochnant. By 1981 the original Morris garage in Pentrefelin had been sold and the bus company had become Tanat Valley Coaches.

Deregulation in October 1986 brought further opportunities and a chance to compete with Crosville on more equal terms. Tanat Valley introduced their own weekday route from Llangynog, Pentrefelin, and Llanrhaeadr-ym-Mochnant to Oswestry in direct competition with Crosville's (ex-railway) D79 service. The bigger fish seemed almost unaware of this annoying new minnow but its receipts from the Tanat valley route plummeted and in October 1987 Crosville withdrew from the contest.

Since this minor (but highly symbolic) victory the Tanat Valley business has continued to grow at a feverish pace. The Oswestry town operations of Michael Jones' Llansilin Motor Services were acquired in November 1990, followed by the remainder of that business in April 1993. Successful bids for tendered local bus services and schools contracts further boosted the enterprise, and a veritable flood of second-hand vehicles surged into the depot at Llanrhaeadr-ym-Mochnant. The influx included four Alexander-bodied Fords from Highland Omnibuses and numerous Bristol RE saloons and VRT3 double-deckers from assorted ex-NBC subsidiaries. Later arrivals were an eclectic mixture of double-deckers including an Atlantean, several Fleetlines, five Olympians, a Titan, and two Metrobuses, three Marshall-bodied Dennis Lancet saloons from Blackpool, six East Lancs-bodied Tiger single-deckers from Arriva Midlands North, and a couple of Leyland Nationals. By 1996 the fleet had grown to 16 vehicles, by 2000 to 28, and by 2005 to 43. A tiny amount of this spectacular growth came from the acquisition of the business of Morris of Llanfyllin in Montgomeryshire (no relation to the Morrises of Tanat Valley) in October 2000.

Elvin Morris died in 1998 at the age of 90, having witnessed the resurgence of his family business from a single coach operation to become one of the most important providers of local bus services in the region. For some independent bus company proprietors it seems, life really does begin at the age of 65.

Peters of Llanarmon-yn-Lal

Llanarmon-yn-Lal is a medium-sized village in the Alyn valley, to the northwest of Wrexham. The traditional industry of the community was lead-mining, but by 1903 the local mines were exhausted and agriculture and quarrying then became the two main sources of employment in the area. The first motor-bus service to the village began in 1923 when George Edwards of Bwlchgwyn (qv) started a route from Llanarmon-yn-Lal to Wrexham via his home village. This ran on Mondays, Thursdays, and Saturdays, and on Wednesdays Edwards operated a second service from Coedpoeth to Mold via Bwlchgwyn and Llanarmon-yn-Lal. Both routes were scheduled for days when markets were held in the respective towns. Crosville soon arrived on the scene and started an infrequent service from Ruthin to Mold which passed through the village.

At some point in the late 1920s (details are sadly lacking) Mr Robert E Peters of Llanarmon-yn-Lal decided to commence his own market-day services to Mold and Wrexham, suggesting that the Edwards and Crosville routes were doing well and inviting imitation. In 1931 Peters applied for licences for his two routes and for a works service from Llanarmon-yn-Lal to Llay Main colliery. After some wrangling in front of the Traffic Commissioners the Wrexham service was allocated to Edwards (who had an earlier claim as an operator), but Peters received a licence for a Wednesday only service to Mold along with a daily, on demand, works run to Llay Main. He was also granted authorisation for excursions and tours from Llanarmon-yn-Lal and several of the surrounding villages. No details of the company's pre-war vehicles have been discovered, although an old postcard of the village co-incidentally includes what appears to be a Chevrolet bus (probably a 14-seater) in the background. It is clearly not a Crosville machine and doesn't appear to have been owned by Edwards, but it might merely have been visiting Llanarmon-yn-Lal and cannot be definitively identified as a Peters vehicle.

By 1945 the business had passed to the founder's son, Edward Garnett Peters, assisted by his wife Myfanwy. In fact the earliest known Peters vehicle, a new Bedford OB/Duple Vista coach acquired in 1947, was actually registered to Mrs Peters until October 1951 when it was transferred to her husband's ownership. Three more new vehicles followed in 1948 (all registered to EG Peters), presumably eliminating most or all of the pre-war machines before their identities could be recorded by the PSV Circle's roving reporters. The 1948 newcomers were two more OB/Duple Vista coaches and, more unusually, a Burlingham-bodied Foden PVSC6. Further new equipment arrived in 1949 in the shape of another Burlingham-bodied coach (but this time on a Crossley SD42 chassis) and an Austin CXB coach with bodywork by Beccols of Chequerbent. The Peters also treated themselves to a second-hand Riley saloon car which one source claims to have been licensed as a 3-seat PSV!

With the coach fleet renewed at great expense the couple turned to equipment for the bus services. A four year old Foden PVSC5 with 37-seat bus bodywork by Saunders arrived from Crown of Birtley in October 1951 and found employment on the service to Mold and various schools-related contracts. It was followed by two pre-war Leyland 'LT series' Lions with interesting histories. One, CKH 165, had been new to an unidentified Kingston-upon-Hull operator in 1936, but at some point had migrated to Scotland and had been fitted with a (post-war) Alexander body. It came to Peters from Clyde Valley of Motherwell in Lanarkshire. The other, OD 5869, had started life with Devon General in 1933 as a 31-seat Weymann-bodied bus. In 1940 it had been requisitioned for wartime service and transferred to Valliant of Ealing in London. After the war Valliant kept it for a while and gave it a new Harrington coach body. It later served with Davies of Summerhill (qv), Sykes of Sale, and G&S of Hooton before arriving at Llanarmon-yn-Lal. Both Lions were acquired for the Llay Main colliery service, although they sometimes appeared alongside (or instead of) the PVSC5 bus on the market-day route to Mold.

The first new vehicle to arrive for four years was a Bedford SB with a 36-seat Harrington coach body, delivered in June 1953. The Peters were apparently less impressed by the SB than most operators as their next new coach was a Duple-bodied Commer Avenger III which arrived in May 1956. These new vehicles allowed the older coaches to be transferred to the colliery service and the pre-war Lions had both been scrapped by the end of 1957.

A highly unusual machine was acquired in July 1959. TCA 309 was a Crossley SD42/9 with Whitson 'observation coach' bodywork seating 35 passengers. New to the US Air Force at Lakenheath in 1951 as one of ten similar machines acquired for the transportation of military bands and American Football teams, it featured a 'Foden style' full-front and radiator grille which confused

I have no reports of this machine being used on Peters' stage route, but who could resist including it? Despite appearances this is not a Foden but a Crossley SD42/9 masquerading as one, and carries 35-seat Whitson 'observation coach' bodywork. New to the United States Air Force at Lakenheath in 1951, it ran with the USAF serial number N975 until being sold to Peters in July 1959. It was thus first registered in Britain (as TCA 309) when already eight years old. Seen at the depot in Llanarmon-yn-Lal, it was withdrawn from use in February 1962 and tragically scrapped. *(Roy Marshall via the Omnibus Society)*

Photographs of vehicles belonging to the LG Phillips fleet seem to be particularly rare, but here is an atmospheric shot of their premises in Glyn Ceiriog – known locally as 'The Motories'. On the left is Bedford SB3/Duple Super Vega VCA 98, new in March 1960 and carrying a pink and cream livery. On the right is Royal Tiger/Burlingham Seagull ODH 720, acquired from Boult of Walsall in November 1960 and painted in a grey and red colour scheme. *(Geoff Lumb)*

This Crossley Condor, VU 6292, was new to Manchester Corporation in 1931 and was fitted with a 52-seat body made in Manchester's own 'Car Works'. After 16 years with MCTD it was sold to Phillips of Holywell in April 1947. It was eventually withdrawn in February 1950, having achieved a very impressive age for a pre-war Crossley, and might well have been the last of its species in revenue-earning service. *(Author's Collection)*

In July 1949 Phillips bought their first (and only) new double-decker, a Massey-bodied Foden PVD6 registered FDM 724. Neighbouring fleet P & O Lloyd of Bagillt bought an identical machine in the same year, and it is believed that both Fodens were 'added on' to a batch already ordered from Massey Bros by Chester Corporation. In 1969 Phillips' example was sold to Hollis of Queensferry and rotted in their yard until 1980 when it was rescued for preservation. The vehicle is presently housed in the BaMMOT museum at Wythall but still needs a lot of work. *(Peter Harden Collection)*

many enthusiasts. In USAF service it had carried the military serial number N975 and had never been registered in the UK until its arrival in Denbighshire.

The next acquisition, an ageing Dennis Lancet J3/Duple coach, came in April 1960 but was withdrawn after a year and a half. Other departures in 1960/1 included the 1948 Foden PVSC6 and the 1953 Bedford SB. Their replacements were another Duple-bodied Commer coach (an Avenger IV acquired from Yates of Runcorn) and a Leyland Royal Tiger with coach bodywork by Trans-United which came from Leadbetter of Sutton Coldfield. February 1962 saw the demise of the ex-USAF Crossley but its successor softened the blow. MXB 38 was a rare Tilling-Stevens Express Mk II with a Duple 'Vega lookalike' coach body. It came from Banfield in London who had acquired it with the take-over of a smaller operator and had no desire to keep such an unusual specimen.

A second Duple-bodied Avenger IV arrived from another London coach firm (Hall of Hillingdon) in August 1965, and was followed by a brand-new 45-seat Bedford VAM70/Duple coach in October 1968. By then the market-day service to Mold had become a shadow of its former self and on days of bad weather would sometimes run empty in both directions. The Peters reluctantly surrendered the licence on 4th July 1970 and Crosville introduced an extra timing to fill the gap. With the Llay Main works service already gone (after the colliery's closure in 1966) this left the business with just its coaching activities, and the fleet was reduced to two vehicles by the start of 1971, the most recent of the two Commer Avenger IVs and the 1968 VAM70.

Mr Peters retired at the end of the 1970s and the company ceased to trade. The final link to the business was broken in June 2009 when his widow, Mrs Myfanwy Peters, died in a nursing home near Wrexham at the age of 96. In her will she requested that donations (in lieu of funeral flowers) should be sent to an old people's charity in South America. It was an interesting footnote to the story of a fascinating operator.

Phillips of Glyn Ceiriog

The Ceiriog valley, southwest of Wrexham and northwest of Oswestry, has traditionally been sustained by a mixture of livestock farming and slate quarrying. The two major quarries at Glyn Ceiriog and Pandy were at one time connected to the canal system by a horse-drawn tramway. This later evolved into a steam-powered railway, was extended eastwards to connect with mainline trains at Chirk, and carried passengers until its closure in 1935.

In the first two decades of the 20th century vehicles propelled by petrol engines became an increasingly frequent sight in the valley and Haydn Phillips, the sixth child of Elias and Jane Phillips, decided to benefit from the paradigm shift in motive power. Shortly after the end of the First World War he opened a garage and filling station in Glyn Ceiriog (the premises became known locally as 'The Motories'), and as the years went by he added a car dealership, tipper and flatbed lorries, and livestock wagons to his list of assets.

Motor-buses came to the valley in the same decade. Alfred Wright started a service from Chirk, later sold to Bryn Melyn (qv) and extended to Llangollen, while Arthur of Oswestry offered a route from their home town. By 1929 Haydn Phillips had decided to compete for a share of this traffic and bought a 20-seat GMC bus to operate from Llanarmon Dyffryn Ceiriog and Glyn Ceiriog to both Llangollen (on Tuesdays and Fridays) and Oswestry (on Wednesdays and Saturdays).

In 1934 the announcement that the passenger railway line was to close encouraged Phillips to acquire a second vehicle, a 20-seat Bedford WLB. At around the same time the company began to use the fleet-name 'Ceiriog Valley Transport' for its stage carriage operations, although the use of this title was fairly sporadic over the years. The withdrawal of the rail service also created extra demand for private cars and light goods vehicles, resulting in the growth of Phillips' Hillman and Commer dealership. The revenue from this activity was ploughed back into the business and the original garage was replaced by an impressive new structure which resembled a miniature 'Art Deco' cinema.

The bus side of the company also received investment. A second Bedford, a slightly larger WTB coach, was delivered in early 1937 to cater for a newly awarded excursions and tours licence. Pick-up points throughout the Ceiriog valley made such outings a popular option. In August 1939 (a month before the declaration of war with

Germany) another licence was approved, for a 'works' service from the Ceiriog valley villages to the new military camp at Park Hall in Oswestry on six days each week. Arthur of Oswestry received a similar licence and the two operators, previously fierce competitors on the roads between the valley and Oswestry, began to coordinate their efforts in the national interest. In August 1940 Phillips acquired a fourth vehicle, a 27-seat Commer, to help cope with this service and a new contract to carry miners to Black Park colliery.

The GMC was finally withdrawn in 1943 and replaced by a Bedford OWB utility bus. Peacetime brought fresh opportunities as the Traffic Commissioners agreed to integrate the licences for the six days per week service to Park Hall and the market-days only route to Oswestry town centre. Arthur of Oswestry was given an identical new licence for a daily (except Sunday) service from Llanarmon DC to Oswestry and the two operators agreed to cooperate on scheduling. The Arthur business would be merged into that of Vagg of Knockin Heath in 1947, but the agreement would be unaltered by this change of 'Oswestry end' operator.

In 1946 the two pre-war Bedfords were sold to Morris of Llanfyllin in Montgomeryshire and replaced by an early post-war OB with Duple 'Mk II' bus bodywork. Another OB bus, but with Mulliner bodywork, arrived in April 1949 and allowed the Commer to be sold. The fleet was then composed of three Bedford buses (but no coaches), a situation remedied in June 1950 when the wartime OWB was sold and replaced by a second-hand OB/Duple Vista. By this time the founder had passed his 75th birthday but remained active in all aspects of the business.

Haydn Phillips died in 1953 without a clear successor. His son, Gerald, had established a profitable TV and radio dealership in Chirk and had no wish to enter the bus industry so late in his own life. As a temporary measure the business passed into the stewardship of the founder's daughter, Mrs Joan Coutts. Eventually it was decided that the proprietorship would 'skip' a generation and in November 1954 Lesley Gordon Phillips became the new owner. He took stock of the diverse mini-conglomerate he had inherited and made a decision to concentrate on the rather under-developed coaching side of the enterprise.

The company's first 'Big Bedford', an SB/

Duple Vega coach acquired from Auty's Tours of Bury, arrived in March 1955. In 1956/7 the two Bedford OB buses were sold and replaced by two second-hand half-cab coaches, a Daimler CVD6/Burlingham and an AEC Regal III/Harrington. These were deemed to be suitable for either bus or coach work, although by then the Tuesday and Friday service to Llangollen had already ceased in the face of competition from Bryn Melyn's more frequent (and six days per week) service along most of its length.

A third half-cab coach, a Leyland PS2 Tiger with Harrington bodywork, came from a West Midlands operator in July 1958 but was quickly replaced in the following April by a second SB coach. The latter was unusual in having bodywork by Brush (albeit to the Duple Vega design) and a rare Merionethshire registration. This too was a short-term resident at 'The Motories', being replaced in March 1960 by a brand-new SB3/Duple Super Vega coach. Phillips' first underfloor-engined vehicle, a Leyland Royal Tiger with Burlingham's classic Seagull design of coach bodywork, arrived from Boult of Walsall in November 1960. The fleet now included four vehicles; the Royal Tiger (which had replaced the Regal III), the new SB3, the CVD6/Burlingham half-cab, and the Bedford OB coach. The latter two vehicles were the regulars on the Oswestry service, but their increasing age was causing problems and Phillips' workings on the route began to acquire a reputation for unreliability.

To address this problem Mr Phillips paid a visit to the Don Everall dealership in Wolverhampton in August 1961 and traded the OB in against two 'bargain' purchases, an AEC Regal IV/Duple coach and a Sentinel STC4/40 bus. Both suffered from mechanical faults within weeks of their arrival in Glyn Ceiriog and added to the popular perception that Phillips could no longer be trusted to turn up. There are two versions of what happened next. In one version Mr Phillips returned the two vehicles to Don Everall and unilaterally cancelled the hire-purchase agreement which had funded their acquisition as the 'goods' were of 'unmerchantable' quality. In the other (as told by a former Don Everall employee) Phillips failed to make his first payment and the vehicles were repossessed. Whatever the truth of the matter both machines were back in Wolverhampton after less than two months in Glyn Ceiriog.

Even after digital enhancement this remains a poor quality view, but it was still the best of the three shots available of Phillips' two Seddon Mk 4s. FDM 773 was fitted with 31-seat bus bodywork by Seddon themselves and was new to Phillips in November 1949. Seen at the depot, it was withdrawn and scrapped in September 1964. *(Peter Harden Collection)*

The Leyland Comet, usually a lorry chassis, enjoyed brief popularity as the basis for several hundred coaches and less than a dozen buses between 1948 and 1956. Phillips' GDM 407 was new in August 1950 and carried a 33-seat coach body by Burlingham. It was withdrawn in June 1967 and conflicting reports say that it then went to either Jones of Flint or Cotton of Ormskirk. *(Peter Harden Collection)*

A scene at Phillips' Holywell base featuring Metro-Cammell-bodied Leyland PD1 HF 9590 and the back end of Plaxton-bodied Commer Avenger III NDM 573. The PD1 came to Phillips from Wallasey Corporation in February 1959, and was replaced in October 1965 by a PD2 – also acquired from Wallasey. The Avenger was new to Phillips in June 1956. *(Peter Harden Collection)*

Another depot shot, this time starring Phillips' famous Seddon Mk 17 TDM 855, one of the very few of this model built for the British market. The vehicle was new in August 1959 and had a 35-seat bus body also manufactured by Seddon. Most British registered Mk 17s were owned by local authorities as 'welfare buses' (Oldham had one) and this might well have been the only example licensed as a PSV. It was sold in 1970, fate unknown. *(Peter Yeomans)*

The Phillips fleet was now reduced to three vehicles with no possibility of further arrivals until the dispute with Don Everall could be settled. Aware of the situation with their joint operator, Vagg agreed to assume responsibility for the lion's share of the Oswestry service. As the route was actually running at a loss by 1961 this was an act of considerable generosity. In subsequent years Phillips' participation in the service would be limited to two round-trips per week (a Wednesday market-day run and a late night rotation for cinema-goers on Saturdays) along with responsibility for any – rarely required - duplication from the Ceiriog valley end.

The CVD6 was sold for scrap in February 1963, and after a seven month gap (presumably while the company sought a source of finance) was replaced by a third-hand Bedford SBG/Duple Super Vega. In January 1966 the stylish but thirsty Royal Tiger/Seagull was sold, succeeded by an SB3/Super Vega. It should be noted that both the SBG and SB3 models were petrol-engined and by the mid-1960s were often cheaper to buy on the second-hand market than their thriftier diesel cousins. The suspicion that Phillips' credit was severely restricted was reinforced in June 1967 when the company acquired its final 'full-size' vehicle, a 1950 vintage OB/Duple Vista coach which came from Mates of Chirk. It would be replaced by an 11-seat BMC minibus less than a year after its arrival.

Another departure during 1968 was the SBG purchased in 1963, leaving just two SB3/Duple Super Vega coaches and one minibus in the fleet. The end was clearly in sight. In January 1969 the two SB3s were sold to Banwy Valley Transport in Montgomeryshire and the minibus to a local taxi firm. Crosville agreed to assume responsibility for Phillips' remaining journeys on the Llanarmon DC to Oswestry service, a decision they soon came to regret when they realised how little the timings were actually used. People had been left at bus-stops on far too many occasions by the previous operator.

The garage in Glyn Ceiriog continued to operate for another two decades, but eventually closed and became derelict. It was demolished in 2010 to make way for a proposed low-cost housing development. In a few more years the Phillips company will be forgotten by all except those with a liking for the quixotic backwaters of transport history.

Phillips of Holywell

Edward Henry Phillips was born in the Holywell area of northern Flintshire, but later found employment in the engineering department of Birmingham City Tramways. In 1921 he decided to return to his home town to establish a new business with the backing of several relatives. EH Phillips Motor Services started in a modest way with a French built car chassis (one source suggests that it was a Unic taxi) converted to carry up to 10 passengers. Phillips initially specialised in works services from Holywell to Shotton steelworks and to various textile mills in Flint and Greenfield. Within a year he had acquired three military surplus Sunbeam ambulances and had them converted into buses by his uncle, a skilled joiner. The 'do-it-yourself' nature of his makeshift fleet enabled him to offer lower prices than his competitors, and the business soon became a major player in the Flintshire works services market alongside that other famous operator P & O Lloyd of Bagillt.

Unlike his neighbours Phillips decided to diversify into stage carriage services available to the general public. His initial routes were market-day runs into Holywell from the villages of Lixwm, Rhes-y-Cae, and Rhewl (the latter not to be confused with its namesake in the Llangollen area), all situated to the south of the town. A Dennis 30 cwt bus (illustrated in the Introduction) was acquired in 1927 to operate these services. In May 1929 he became bolder and began to compete with Crosville, recently acquired by the almighty LMS Railway, on the route from Holywell to Mold via Halkyn and Rhosesmor. A 31-seat Leyland Lion was acquired from Baxter of Hanley to match the similar vehicles used by the larger company. Crosville met this challenge with 'chaser' buses, which shadowed Phillips' timings, and Phillips then retaliated by introducing new services to Pantasaph and Whitford, villages to the west of Holywell already served by Crosville.

The corporate giant and the plucky local businessman were forced to the negotiating table by the Road Traffic Act of 1930 and the arrival of the regulated era. It was eventually agreed that all of Phillips' 'village services' would pass to Crosville, and that in exchange Phillips would receive a 50% share of the more important route to Mold. As the service was hourly this meant that Phillips operated once every two hours, and although this might only require one vehicle at off-peak times, duplicates were frequently necessary – especially on market-days at both ends of the route.

New vehicles delivered during this era included a 20-seat Dennis G in 1930, a 34-seat Dennis Lancet in 1932, and a Lancet Mk II in 1936. Phillips also acquired a second-hand 32-seat Dennis E from A1 Services in Ayrshire, a 34-seat Daimler from a Staffordshire operator, and a second Leyland Lion (this one of the longer PLSC3 variety) from Birkenhead Corporation. The PLSC3 would be the first of many vehicles to be acquired from Wirral peninsula municipal operators.

The start of the Second World War in 1939 brought a large increase in demand for Phillips' works services. To cater for this upsurge in traffic a new Commer 32-seater arrived in January 1940 and other wartime purchases included four Bedfords (second-hand examples of the WLB and WTB plus two OWB utility buses), two Leyland Lions from Maidstone & District, and two Leyland Lionesses which had been new to Crosville but came to Phillips from another Flintshire independent, Wakley of Northop.

The first post-war acquisition was a former Biddulph & District Leyland Lion which arrived from North Western in October 1946. In March of the following year a Dennis Lancet came from the same source, but the big news of 1947 was the arrival of Phillips' first two double-deckers. VU 6292, a Crossley Condor, had been new to Manchester while BG 475, a Leyland TD1 Titan with Massey bodywork, came from Birkenhead. They were joined, in November 1948, by a single-deck AEC Regal bus acquired from Chester Corporation.

The double-deckers had become a necessity to avoid duplication on the route to Mold, and the rapid increase in traffic on this service helped to pay for a major fleet renewal programme during 1949. Five new vehicles arrived during that year; two Dennis Lancet J3s with Santus coach bodywork, two Seddon Mk 4 single-decker buses, and a Foden PVD6 double-decker with Massey bodywork. P & O Lloyd of Bagillt bought an identical Foden at the same time. Phillips' PVD6 replaced their Crossley Condor, while the TD1 Titan acquired from Birkenhead in 1947

was replaced by a slightly newer (and Leyland bodied) TD2 version from the same municipality in May 1949.

A pair of new Burlingham-bodied Leyland coaches arrived in 1950. Both were 33-seaters but one was a 'forward control' PS1 Tiger half-cab and the other a 'bonneted' CPO1 Comet. Traffic on the Mold route continued to increase and in 1951 two more second-hand double-deckers arrived to assist the shiny PVD6 and the slightly decrepit TD2. The first to enter service was a TD4c Titan with Metro-Cammell bodywork bought from Wallasey Corporation, the second a Massey-bodied TD7c from Chester.

In July 1953 the surviving OWB was replaced by a three year old OB/Mulliner bus acquired from Owen Brothers of Rhostyllen. Passenger figures on the Mold service were now declining and many off-peak journeys and short-workings to Halkyn were operated by the OB and the two Seddon Mk 4s. With less need for double-deckers the pre-war 'TD' Titans were phased out and by the end of 1956 the Foden was the only example left in the fleet. The founder's health was now failing and in the mid-1950s some of the works contracts (and several vehicles, including the OB bus) were transferred to younger members of the family who established a separate business based at Bagillt. After Edward Henry Phillips' death in 1957 the original company in Holywell passed to his widow, Lydia, and one of his sons, Henry Owen Phillips – known as Harry. Both had played active roles in the business for many years.

As the PVD6 grew older it required more frequent maintenance (don't we all?) and a second double-decker became necessary to act as a 'back up' vehicle. In 1958 two PD1 Titans with Metro-Cammell bodywork were acquired from Wallasey. The better of the two entered service while the other became a source of spares. On the single-deck front, one of the Seddon Mk 4s was retired in the summer of 1959. Its replacement was another Seddon, a rare Mk 17 with 35-seat bus bodywork also manufactured by Seddon.

During the 1960s the ageing coaches in the fleet were replaced by a variety of new Bedfords including a pair of SBs with Burlingham Gannet bodywork and another equipped with the successor Duple (Northern) company's Firefly design. Double-deckers were all second-hand and all from Wallasey; another PD1/Met-Cam

Moving southwards to the Wrexham area, Phillips of Rhostyllen received this Mulliner-bodied Bedford OB bus when new in December 1949. FUJ 219 came from the Greenhous dealership, hence the Shropshire registration. Withdrawn by Phillips in January 1961, it was next reported as a mobile shop in the Whittle-le-Woods area of Lancashire in November 1966. *(Roy Marshall via the Omnibus Society)*

This 36-seat Mulliner-bodied SB, HAW 845, was also new to Phillips via the Greenhous Bedford dealership. Delivered in September 1951, it was sold to Parish of Morda in May 1963. The vast majority of Mulliner-bodied SBs were sold to 'non-PSV' customers including the armed forces, government agencies, and airport authorities, although some of these later found their way to bus operators. *(Roy Marshall via the Omnibus Society)*

Phillips' next SB bus, KUX 435 (another Greenhous supplied machine), arrived in May 1954 and had 40-sea
Duple bodywork. It is seen here in Wrexham bus station with Wright of Penycae's Wulfrunian waiting behind i
Both vehicles are bound for the Rhosllanerchrugog area – abbreviated to 'Rhos' on the Bedford's destination blin
(Roy Marshall via Ray Jones)

Phillips was another recipient of a former Stratford Blue PS1 Tiger/NCB bus, in this case GUE 251 which arrived a
Rhostyllen in February 1961. It survived until May 1966 and was not replaced by another bus as fewer duplicate
were required by that time. *(Roy Marshall via Tony Beasley)*

August 1961 and two PD2s with Burlingham odywork in October 1965. Only one of the latter air entered service.

Two Bedford VAM coaches replaced the last f the half-cabs in 1966 and proved reliable nough to bring about a change in policy for us purchases. A new VAM with 45-seat Duple Midland) bus bodywork arrived in 1967 and ecame the front-line vehicle on the service to Mold, backed up by the PVD6. The faithful Foden vas finally retired in 1969 and sold to Hollis of Queensferry. After a long period of deterioration n Hollis's yard it was rescued for preservation nd currently resides in the BaMMOT museum at Wythall in Worcestershire.

The Foden's replacement was a third eneration Seddon, a Pennine Mk IV with 44-eat bus bodywork, which joined the VAM bus n the Mold route in August 1969. Phillips was e only British operator to acquire new Seddon SV models which had been launched in all three ecades of the post-war era (1940s/50s/60s), and e notoriously poor quality of the Pennine RU nodel ensured that such a claim could never be ade in the future. A much more widely praised ingle-decker entered service in June 1970 in the hape of a PSUC1/2 Tiger Cub with Burlingham eagull coach bodywork. New to Ribble in 1956 had actually been acquired by Phillips in May 968, but had received a full refurbishment o restore it to virtually 'as new' condition. Unsurprisingly, it passed to another operator after isposal by Phillips and survives to the present ay in preservation.

Mrs Phillips passed away in the early 1970s nd ownership of the business was transferred to new partnership of Henry Owen Phillips and is two sons, John and Anthony. An interesting rrival under the new regime was a 35-seat Bristol C4LK/ECW bus acquired from Lincolnshire Road Car Co in August 1976. This abomination nly lasted for 12 months despite the acquisition f a second example for use as a source of spares. third-hand Bedford YRQ/Willowbrook bus, vhich came from Mowbray of Stanley (County Durham) in 1980, proved to have more staying ower.

In 1981 Crosville decided to close its depot n nearby Flint and found itself in the somewhat mbarrassing position of having to base five of its ehicles at Phillips' yard in Holywell. A further

sign of the times came in 1983/4, when Phillips bought four 1975 vintage Bristol LH/ECW buses from the state-owned operator and assumed sole responsibility for the service to Mold along with several 'village' routes abandoned by Crosville. The Chester-based company had used the route number 'B26' for the Holywell to Mold service and Phillips continued to use this for a while before redesignating the route as the '126'.

Despite some new competitors Phillips continued to thrive in the deregulated age. In November 1997 the partnership was replaced by a corporate entity, Phillips Coaches Holywell Ltd, and in January 2005 another company, EH Phillips Motor Services Ltd, was registered with Anthony Phillips and Leslie Williams as its directors. This latter company apparently remained dormant until October 2008 when it acquired the assets and services of the earlier (1997) limited company and began to trade as 'Phillips Coaches'. By then Anthony Phillips had retired, but the business continues to use the widely respected Phillips name for both local bus services and an extensive coaching programme.

Phillips of Rhostyllen

John Phillips left school in an age when motor vehicles were still a rarity and his first few jobs were at the reins of horse-drawn conveyances whilst in the employ of Wrexham Corporation, a salt merchant, and the local railway company. After saving a large proportion of his meagre wages he bought his own horse and cart and used it to deliver coal to domestic consumers, but the First World War intervened before he could reap the benefits of his enterprise. Rather than wait for conscription he voluntarily joined the Royal Flying Corps and by doing so avoided the mass slaughter in the trenches.

The RFC was undoubtedly attracted by the young recruit's skill with horses, but the British military was in a period of transition to motor vehicles, and while enlisted he learned to drive the newfangled machines and became adept enough at their maintenance to keep them on the road. Like many other Wrexham area residents with similar training, he returned from wartime service with a small demobilisation payment and an ambition to start his own business. A taxi was duly acquired and put to work on the route between Wrexham and its largest 'satellite' village, Rhosllanerchrugog – commonly known as 'Rhos' for obvious reasons. Phillips later extended his version of the route to Rhos Tainant, a mile or so beyond the village.

By the late 1920s he had purchased his first two small buses, believed to be Chevrolets, and his son Hugh (born in 1909) had joined the business as a second driver. The Road Traffic Act of 1930 introduced a new level of financial security for those, like Phillips, who were fortunate enough to receive licences, and enabled the purchase of newer, larger, vehicles. A 20-seat Bedford WLB was acquired in 1934, and a second in early 1935. Phillips' next vehicle, a 26-seat Leyland SKP Cub with coach bodywork by Spicer, arrived later in 1935 and its comfortable seating made it an instant success in the local private-hire market.

Phillips, however, preferred the simplicity of the Bedford engine and his next coach was a Duple-bodied WTB delivered in 1936. A second WTB replaced the Cub in 1937. Meanwhile, the WLBs were struggling to cope with demand on the stage carriage service, and in 1938 the older of the two was traded in for a 35-seat Tilling-Stevens bus which promised to pay for itself by eliminating duplication and a second driver's wages. The private-hire and excursion business was also booming and in June 1939 two more WTB/Duple coaches arrived to cope with this traffic. Three months later the country was at war again and the new coaches were soon carrying military personnel rather than day-trippers.

Much of Phillips' wartime work involved long-distance military contracts and in November 1940 a fifth (second-hand) WTB was allocated to the company for these services, taking local conscripts to training camps around the country and those already trained from their last brief periods of leave to seaports or domestic barracks. The Wrexham area's coalmines were also essential to the war effort in an era when most of the country's trains and nearly all of its naval vessels still used coal-fuelled steam power. In March 1943 a Bedford OWB utility bus arrived to take some of the pressure away from the (frequently drastically overloaded) Tilling-Stevens. By the end of the war the entire Phillips fleet stood in dire need of replacement, although – as most of its patriotic work had been undertaken at cost or slightly below – the firm's finances were in equally poor condition.

A solution was found when Vincent Greenhous, a Shrewsbury based dealer with a branch i Wrexham, offered an attractive hire-purchas arrangement. As a result all but one of Phillips new vehicles delivered between 1947 and 195 would be registered in Shropshire rather than th company's native Denbighshire. The first to arriv was an OB/Duple Vista coach in March 1947. was followed by an OB/Mulliner bus in Januar 1948, another OB/Vista coach in January 1949 and two more OB/Mulliner buses in late 1949 an June 1950. The older vehicles they replaced a went to Greenhous for re-sale, with many findin new owners in Shropshire or Herefordshir (where Greenhous had another branch). Th OWB was among the exceptions and was sold t the neighbouring firm of Johnson of Southsea (qv in February 1950.

Two Bedford SB/Duple Vega coaches arrive in May and June 1951, followed by a 36-seat SE Mulliner bus in September of that year. A simila vehicle, but with 40-seat bus bodywork built a Duple's new Kegworth factory (the former Nud Bros & Lockyer), arrived in May 1954. Furthe SB/Duple coaches came in 1956/8/9 to update th private-hire and excursion fleet.

By this time the founder had departed, Hug Phillips was the proprietor, and in view of th declining traffic on the stage service he decided t replace the OB/Mulliner buses with two second hand purchases. Both were Leyland PS1 Tigers a BBW-bodied example which came from Re & White in August 1959 (Bryn Melyn took a identical vehicle), and a Northern Coach Builder specimen acquired from Stratford Blue in Januar 1961 (one of four from that company which ende up with North Wales stage carriage operators including one with fellow Wrexham independen Chaloner of Moss).

The first of the SB buses was the next t go, sold to Parish of Morda (via Greenhous) i May 1963 and replaced by a new SB5/Dupl (Midland) saloon. A second vehicle of this typ came in March 1964 and succeeded the Re & White PS1 Tiger. The newer buses brough increased reliability, and as a result the 1954 SI bus and the Stratford Blue PS1 were traded in fo a second-hand SB/Duple Super Vega coach i March 1966. A new 29-seat Bedford VAS/Dupl coach arrived in August 1967, but the followin three coaches would all be second-hand Bedfor

Williams of Ponciau acquired its Rhostyllen route with the business of Owen of that village in 1952. Williams' Mulliner-bodied OB bus, FUN 310, is seen on stand three at Wrexham bus station awaiting departure. New in March 1949, it was withdrawn from use in June 1960. *(Roy Marshall via Peter Harden)*

Williams caused something of a stir in the Wrexham area in May 1951 when it acquired this almost new AEC Regal IV with 41-seat bus bodywork by Charles H Roe of Leeds. DHL 166 had appeared on the Roe stand at the 1950 Commercial Motor Show in West Riding livery, complete with fleet number 706, but never operated in revenue-earning service for the Wakefield company. After 16 years with Williams the vehicle was sold to Mid-Wales Motorways in May 1966, remaining in service until January 1972. It was scrapped in May 1973. *(David Cunningham)*

Maudslay Marathon GGD 724 came to Williams from Northern Roadways in March 1952 and carried a 33-seat coach body made by Duple. Despite its luxurious seating it spent most of its time as a duplicate on the service from Wrexham to Rhosllanerchrugog – a far cry from its original role as a long distance express vehicle. *(Roy Marshall via Ray Jones)*

In October 1956 Williams bought a pair of Crossley SD42 buses with 35-seat Crossley bodies, MLF 347/8, previously operated by Mollins Machinery. Mollins made tobacco processing equipment and had used the vehicles as staff buses in the southeast London/northwest Kent area. Another former Mollins Crossley passed to Fisher of Bronington two years later. MLF 348 is seen shortly after arrival (and still in 'dealer white' with mismatched side panels) on Williams' Rhostyllen route. *(DJ Stanier)*

VAMs bought in 1969/70. The next new vehicle was a Ford R192/Willowbrook service bus and, given Phillips' obvious enthusiasm for the VAM chassis, something of a surprise. It replaced the older of the two SB5/Duple (Midland) buses.

Hugh Phillips had no willing and able successor and a tentative approach to Crosville had been made as early as 1969 when he was approaching his 60th birthday. At that time Crosville's offer (the NBC subsidiary was only interested in the stage service) was seen as far too low and the Phillips company retained its independence for the best part of another decade. A deal was finally agreed as the proprietor entered his 70th year, and the Wrexham route passed to Crosville for an undisclosed sum in 1978. The coaching licences and three vehicles were sold separately to Elias Jones of Rhosllanerchrugog, acting as a seed for the much more significant post-deregulation activities of the Jones family. Hugh Phillips then retired from the bus industry but continued to be active in the affairs of Wrexham football club, of which he was a director and (for many years) the chairman.

Sugg of Garden Village – see Keeler of Garden Village

Tanat Valley Coaches – see Morris of Pentrefelin

Williams of Maerdy

The village of Maerdy is situated on the A5, a few miles to the west of the small Merionethshire town of Corwen and to the south of the village of Bettws Gwerfil Goch, also in Merionethshire. The traditional (pre-1974) county boundaries followed the river, however, and Maerdy itself was on the western (Denbighshire) bank of the River Alwen.

A bus service from Melin-y-Wig and Bettws GG to Corwen began in the mid-1920s, operated by Frederick G Travis of 'Maes Gwerfil'. No other details are known of the early days, but in 1932 Mr Travis received a licence to continue his existing route which operated on Fridays (market-day) and 'Corwen Fair Days' – usually the third Tuesday in each month. Travis's only recorded vehicle, a 1927 Albion 20-seater registered TU

6197, was acquired from Pye of Colwyn Bay in October 1938. Its Cheshire registration reflected Pye's origin as a Cheshire operator before its stage services in the English county were sold to Crosville.

Travis's route was essentially a shopping service and as such of no use to workers employed at the grain mill in Bettws GG. The mill-owners, the Lloyd Davies family, had employees from many of the remote villages in the area and approached a local coach operator to provide a vehicle to collect these workers. The contract went to William John Williams of Maerdy, trading as Grey Motors, a fleet-name probably intended to cock a snook at Crosville which had long been nicknamed 'The Greys' in a reference to its original livery rather than any belief that the company was involved in alien abductions. Those who have seen a photograph of Crosland Taylor may still doubt this explanation.

In October 1949 the Travis route was abandoned without warning (the 22 year old Albion was sold for scrap in the same month which might provide a clue to the reason for this unusual dereliction of an operator's duty) and Crosville was granted a temporary dispensation to provide a replacement service. A 'substantive' licence was granted later in the same year, but Crosville was not alone in seeking to obtain the route. In November 1950 Griffith Richard Williams and Leslie Thomas Russell Williams, trading as Williams Coaches, made an almost identical application to the Traffic Commissioners. The two men were, respectively, the son and grandson of the Grey Motors proprietor and had taken over the Bettws GG mill contract.

The Williams' application was for a service on Mondays, Fridays, and 'Corwen Fair Days', and thus offered more travel opportunities than Crosville's replacement for the original Travis operation. Williams Coaches also applied for an express service from Melin-y-Wig, Bettws GG, and Maerdy to Ruthin, involving a single return journey on 'Ruthin Fair Days'. Crosville objected to both applications, but particularly to the Corwen route which it had already operated for more than a year. Williams Coaches retaliated by appealing against the award of a licence for the Corwen route to Crosville in late 1949.

The various applications were heard by the Traffic Commissioners in the spring of 1951 and resulted in a surprising outcome. The Williams were granted their two licences to Corwen and Ruthin, the former in direct competition with the Crosville route. On the down side, Williams' application to have the Crosville licence revoked was refused in August 1951 and both 'David' and 'Goliath' continued to operate between Melin-y-Wig and Corwen. There appears to have been little (if any) profit to be made by Williams, as in October 1952 the company established a second base at Bethesda in Caernarvonshire in an attempt to generate more private-hire income. It seems that Mr Williams Sr remained in Maerdy while his son moved to Bethesda.

Details of the Williams Coaches fleet in this period are few and far between, and only two vehicles have been identified from PSV Circle records. JTE 967 was a Leyland PS1 Tiger with a fully-fronted 33-seat coach body by Beccols of Chequerbent, while CUN 858 was a Bedford OWB. The latter machine had been new to Phillips of Rhostyllen (qv) in March 1943 with 32 wooden seats, replaced after the war with 30 upholstered ones. In March 1950 it passed to Johnson of Southsea (qv) and then to Williams in February 1956. The OWB was based at the Maerdy end of the operation to cover the mill-workers contract and the two Melin-y-Wig stage carriage routes. A third timetabled service was approved by the Traffic Commissioners in September 1956, an express route from the Alwen valley to Wrexham which operated fortnightly on alternate Thursdays. This licence was later amended at Williams' own request, and the service reduced to operate only on the last Monday in each month.

In April 1959 Williams' licences for the Melin-y-Wig to Corwen and Ruthin services were voluntarily surrendered, leaving the monthly run from the Alwen valley to Wrexham as the company's only scheduled route available to the general public. Henceforth, all vehicles (including that used on the Wrexham run) would be based at Bethesda although the company continued to offer private-hire and other coaching services in Maerdy and the upper Alwen valley until 1978. The further history of this operator from April 1959 until its eventual demise in 1981 can thus be found under the heading of 'Williams of Bethesda' in Part One of this book.

An interesting sequel can be found to this story. The mill-owners at Bettws GG still needed to get their workers to their remote facility. After the Williams' departure for greener pastures Crosville proved unwilling to assume responsibility for this contract and no other local coach firm could be found to operate the service at a reasonable price. As a result John Lloyd Davies bought an 11-seat Morris minibus to carry his employees and later began to offer the vehicle for private-hire work.

Other minibuses followed at regular intervals although only one was owned at any given time. Meanwhile, the mill-owner's son, Eifion Lloyd Davies, had declined to join the family business and had founded his own scrap metal firm known as Auto Spares. After his father's retirement he moved his scrap business into the mill at Bettws GG and also assumed responsibility for the minibus operation, which had by then secured a schools contract to replace its former 'in house' duties.

Eifion Davies decided that the minibus business needed a 'proper' title and named it in honour of his three sons; Gareth, Hefin, and Arwyn. In the new world after deregulation GHA Coaches expanded at a meteoric pace, going from one Mercedes minibus in 1985 to seven vehicles (most of them full-sized coaches) in 1995. By 2001 there were 35 vehicles, and by 2011 more than 200. Along the way GHA had acquired such well-known businesses as Hanmer of Southsea, Vale of Llangollen Travel, Chaloner of Moss (qv), and Bryn Melyn Motor Services (qv). Some of these acquisitions retained their own identities as wholly-owned subsidiaries of GHA.

The company is now one of the largest providers of tendered local bus services in North Wales, with its area of operation spilling over into Shropshire and Cheshire, but none of this would have happened if the Williams had continued to maintain a base in Maerdy. Great oaks can come from very small acorns.

Williams of Ponciau

In North Wales Thomas is one of the three most popular given names and Williams one of the three top surnames, so the combination of the two creates a distinct possibility of confusion. To overcome this problem (and similar ones involving the surnames Jones, Owen, and Roberts) the Welsh are fond of attaching nicknames to individuals as an aid to identification. The family of the Thomas

Williams' Crossley MLF 348 again, but now repainted into the operator's blue and cream livery. The two Crossleys were withdrawn from use in 1964 and after standing in the yard for several years were sold to Gittins, a Wrexham based contractor, for use as 'site huts'. *(TG Turner)*

Between 1961 and 1964 Williams bought four new Bedford SB5/Duple (Midland) buses, replacing all of the stage carriage fleet except for the Regal IV. This is the 1963 machine, 6999 UN, which was replaced in its turn by a new Plaxton-bodied Ford R192 service bus in March 1973. *(Author's Collection)*

Most of Williams' Ford service buses carried Plaxton bodywork, but the first of the breed carried a 45-seat unit manufactured by Willowbrook. TUN 555J was an R192 which arrived in 1971 and is seen here on the Rhostyllen service. *(DJ Stanier)*

By November 1976, when SLG 882R came to Williams, the Ford R192 had become the Ford R1014. It is believed that this vehicle (and a Bedford YNT/Duple bus delivered in 1983) were registered at Chester to reflect their ownership by a Cheshire based leasing company. The Ford carried Plaxton Derwent bodywork and remained in service until Williams abandoned local bus services in 1986. *(DJ Stanier)*

Williams later involved in the Wrexham area bus industry came from Caernarvonshire, so he became known as 'Tommy Caernarvon'.

Williams had followed the family tradition of employment in the coal industry, working as a borer at the Hafod pit until failing health, caused by the coal dust, forced him to seek work above ground. Fortunately, his wife's sister's husband, Samuel Owen, had just the thing. Owen had started a taxi business running between Rhostyllen and Wrexham town centre in 1921, and by 1923 had made enough money to buy a 14-seat bus. This made one of his two cars redundant, so in 1924 he sold it to Williams and taught him how to drive.

In a classic example of biting the hand that fed him Williams responded to this generosity by starting to compete with Owen on the Rhostyllen route, a move that went down very poorly with most of the extended family. Rhostyllen was a relatively small community (and its proximity to the Wrexham & District company's tramway further reduced traffic on the route), hence John Phillips' decision to start a service from Rhosllanerchrugog rather than from his home village. In 1925 Tommy Caernarvon succumbed to pressure from his relatives and switched his vehicle to the Rhosllanerchrugog route. The 'Rhos' area had far more traffic potential but also far more competition. As well as the bus services operated by the tramway company (later inherited by Western Transport and then Crosville), the route was already occupied by Evans of Wrexham (qv), Phillips of Rhostyllen (qv), and Wright of Penycae (qv), among others.

Nevertheless, Williams managed to make a go of it by operating on six days per week. The tramway company only ran on Thursdays, Saturdays, and Sundays, expecting 'Rhos' residents to walk to the tramway terminus on the remaining days. Wright's service was restricted to Mondays, Thursdays, and Saturdays, as he operated a market-day service to Oswestry on Wednesdays and used the same vehicle to deliver coal on Tuesdays, and Fridays. Evans soon withdrew to concentrate on services to the east of Wrexham, leaving Phillips and Williams as the two main operators.

By 1928 Williams had acquired his first 'proper' bus, a 14-seat REO, and this was followed by a Chevrolet of similar size. Both were second-hand but in good enough condition

to earn Williams a route licence in 1931. More second-hand buses followed in the early 1930s including two 20-seat REO variants and two 20-seat Bedford WLBs. Williams' first new vehicle, a 26-seat Bedford WTB bus, was delivered in 1936. A 32-seat Leyland Tiger coach joined the fleet in 1937, and another new WTB – this one a coach – in 1939.

The only wartime acquisition was an OWB utility bus which arrived in 1944. The next new deliveries were of an OB/Duple Vista coach in July 1948, an OB/Mulliner bus in March 1949, and a Plaxton-bodied Crossley SD42 coach in May 1949. They replaced the surviving examples of the REO and WLB and the bus-bodied WTB. In May 1951 a much larger vehicle was painted in Williams' blue and cream livery. DHL 166 was an underfloor-engined AEC Regal IV with a 42-seat bus body by Charles Roe of Leeds. It had been exhibited on the Roe stand at the 1950 Commercial Motor Show in West Riding colours, complete with fleet number 706, but had never actually entered revenue-earning service with the Wakefield company. It replaced Williams' wartime OWB.

The pre-war Tiger coach departed in March 1952, its place taken by a post-war Maudslay Marathon/Duple coach acquired from the Scottish operator Northern Roadways. A more important purchase in October of that year was the business of Owen of Rhostyllen, returning the original route back into Williams' portfolio and laying the ghost of the family feud of the mid-1920s. The deal included an OWB and another OB/Mulliner bus, but the OWB was soon sold leaving the two OB buses to work the Rhostyllen route while the flagship Regal IV maintained the all-day service to Rhosllanerchrugog.

Since the beginning of the company Williams had also operated a works service from 'Rhos' to Llay Main colliery, and in January 1955 a pre-war TS7 Tiger bus was acquired to cover this commitment. It had been new to Crosville who had replaced its original body with an ECW unit in the late 1940s. The vehicle's stay in Ponciau was brief as in 1956 it was replaced by two Crossley SD42 buses acquired from Mollins Machinery. Mollins made machines which made cigarettes and had used the buses (which had Crossley bodywork as well as chassis and engines) as staff buses in the Kent/London border area. Another of Mollins'

Crossleys came to North Wales two years later, operating for Fisher of Bronington (qv).

Tommy Caernarvon died in 1957 and control of the business passed to his sons, Selwyn and Foster Williams. Under their joint proprietorship (still trading as T Williams & Sons) the company began to modernise its fleet. Williams' final pre-war vehicle, the 1939 WTB coach, was retired in early 1958 and replaced by a Bedford SB. More SB coaches would follow to succeed the OB coach, the Plaxton-bodied Crossley, and the Maudslay Marathon. The first of several new SB/Duple (Midland) buses arrived in 1960, and another in 1961, to replace the OB/Mulliners on the Rhostyllen service. Three more came in 1963/4 and replaced the 1960 example (which went to Bryn Melyn) and the two Mollins Crossleys (which were sold to a Wrexham contractor to re-enter the world of non-PSV staff buses).

By 1965 the relentless rise in car ownership had reduced the requirement for duplicate vehicles, and the Bedford VAM/Duple (Midland) bus delivered at the end of that year replaced both the Roe-bodied Regal IV (which passed to Mid-Wales Motorways for a further six years of service) and the 1961 SB bus (which went to Deiniolen Motors in Caernarvonshire). The closure of Llay Main colliery also reduced the company's peak vehicle requirement.

Williams' private-hire and excursion fleet was refreshed in 1967 by the addition of a two year old Bedford SB5/Duple Bella Vega and a brand-new VAM/Duple (Northern) coach. Surprisingly, the next new bus, in January 1969, was not a second VAM but yet another SB. It replaced one of the 1963/4 trio. As will be noted, Williams' stage carriage fleet had developed an astonishingly 'young' age profile during the 1960s – the relative cheapness of the utilitarian SB/Duple (Midland) design had made such a purchasing policy a viable proposition. The 1969 vehicle, however, proved to be the last of its kind bought new by Williams. The next new service bus, acquired in March 1973, was a Ford R192 with Plaxton Derwent bodywork.

Two more Fords with Plaxton bus bodywork followed, a new machine delivered in November 1976, and a second-hand example acquired from Excelsior of Wrockwardine Wood (Shropshire) in August 1981. A more unusual purchase came in December 1981 when UKH 170W arrived in Ponciau. This was a Bedford YMT with the prototype of Plaxton's Bustler body, equipped with 55 seats. It had previously been used by the Scarborough bodybuilder as a demonstrator. Williams' final new service bus came in October 1983, another Bedford but on this occasion with 53-seat Duple Dominant bodywork.

Foster Williams had died in 1981 and with deregulation on the horizon Selwyn Williams decided that the new environment was not to his liking. In September 1986 the venerable old firm of T Williams & Sons withdrew from stage carriage services and sold its remaining buses. The business continued as a coach operator for some time but would show no interest in tendering for bus work.

Phillips of Rhostyllen had already sold its Rhosllanerchrugog service to Crosville in 1978, so Williams' decision left Wright of Penycae as the solitary survivor of the pioneering local firms on the busy road from 'Rhos' to Wrexham. Before too long Wright would also disappear. It was the end of one exciting era and (for younger enthusiasts) the beginning of another.

Wright of Penycae

Alfred Wright of Rhosymedre used his demobilisation gratuity to buy a second-hand Ford Model T lorry-bus, and by 1923 had developed a daily (except Sunday) route from Chirk to Glyn Ceiriog along with various works services in the Chirk and Cefn Mawr area. In 1928 he sold the Glyn Ceiriog route to Bryn Melyn of Llangollen (qv), but kept the works journeys until March 1939 when some passed to Crosville and others to Roberts Coaches of Cefn Mawr. At that point Alfred withdrew from the bus and coach industry.

His brother, Edmund Wright, would establish a firm which made a much more significant contribution to the history of bus services in the Wrexham area. Edmund was a coalminer who lived in the village of Penycae, to the southwest of Wrexham, and after watching Alfred prove that a living could be made from bus services he decided that this option would provide his son, Charles, with a healthier future than the colliery could offer.

In 1924 Edmund bought his own Ford Model T lorry-bus, set Charles to work as its full-time driver, and the pair began to trade as Edmund Wright & Son, bus proprietors and coal merchants. On six days per week the Ford would carry miners from Penycae and Rhosllanerchrugog to and from the Llay Main colliery. Between these journeys the vehicle had a varied schedule. On Mondays, Thursdays, and Saturdays it operated a stage service to Wrexham, on Tuesdays and Fridays it delivered coal, and on Wednesdays it carried passengers to Oswestry market.

The coal merchant side of the business was initially the most successful, and two Vulcan lorries were acquired in 1925/6 to enable both a geographical expansion and the provision of deliveries on days when the Ford was in bus configuration. By 1928 it became necessary to replace this hard-working vehicle with something less begrimed by coal-dust and the Wrights acquired their first 'proper' bus, a 14-seat REO Speedwagon.

With a new purpose-built bus on the premises (and hire-purchase payments to make) it was decided to discontinue the Oswestry service and to apply to the new Traffic Commissioners for a daily route from Penycae to Wrexham. Objections were raised by all of the other operators on the busy sector between Rhosllanerchrugog and the town centre, and the Wrights were eventually licensed for their existing Monday, Thursday, and Saturday timetable only. This was undoubtedly a disappointment, but the coal business was doing well and the REO just about paid for itself when the revenues from the Llay Main journeys were added to those from the Wrexham route.

Passenger traffic increased steadily and by 1938 the REO was both slightly antiquated and no longer adequate in terms of capacity. Its replacement was a brand-new Dodge SBF bus, BCA 367, with 26-seat bodywork by Grose. This vehicle recovered its purchase price several times over while with Wrights, particularly during the war years when it frequently operated up to four round-trips per day to the Llay Main colliery.

In the immediate post-war era the public wanted coach outings and in 1948 Wrights set out to help meet this demand by acquiring a brand-new Bedford OB/Duple Vista coach. The stage carriage service was also due for an update, and in 1949 the Dodge was replaced by a bus-bodied OB/Mulliner. After leaving Wrights BCA 367 went to a private-hire operator in Rhosllanerchrugog for use on a schools contract and then, in 1952, to Ashley of Dawley (in Shropshire). Ashley used it on their daily services in the Wellington area until 1955 and then sold it for further use as a van and mobile shop.

Edmund Wright died in 1952 and the business became Charles Wright, trading as Wrights Coaches. The coal merchant part of the company was then sold to Elias Jones of Rhosllanerchrugog, whose sons would later become bus and coach proprietors themselves. The money from Jones was used to buy a new 35-seat Bedford SB coach with Burlingham 'Seagull lookalike' bodywork in 1953, increasing the PSV fleet to three vehicles. Meanwhile, the company had finally received permission to operate the Penycae to Wrexham service on a daily basis, albeit with restrictions which prohibited local traffic on the 'Rhos' to Wrexham part of the route except on the original three days of operation.

In 1959 Charles' son Michael Wright joined the business as did a fourth new vehicle, a Commer Avenger IV with a two-stroke TS3 diesel engine and 41-seat coach bodywork by Burlingham. A second brand-new Avenger IV coach, but with much more attractive bodywork by Plaxton, arrived in June 1962 and replaced the 1953 Bedford SB. The next newcomer was a six year old Commer T48/Beadle Rochester coach which was acquired from Avis Coaches of London in June 1963. Having a front entrance it was deemed acceptable for stage carriage work and replaced the OB/Mulliner bus on the Wrexham service.

The T48's stay in Penycae would be brief. In August 1964 it went to Howell & Withers in southern Wales as a direct trade for a much more impressive vehicle. LEN 101 was a 73-seat Guy Wulfrunian/Roe double-decker and one of the very few of its kind built for customers other than the type's original sponsor, West Riding. An exhibit at the 1960 Commercial Motor Show, its original purchaser had been Bury Corporation. Unimpressed by their solitary 'Wulf' (as most customers were) Bury sold it to a dealer after less than three years and it then passed to Howell & Withers. They painted it in their grey and white livery but after less than a year were also anxious to get rid of the machine.

Wrights' colour scheme, since the 1938 Dodge, had been two shades of blue (officially described as 'Naples Blue' and 'Circassian Blue'), but the Wulfrunian entered service in a hybrid livery of blue, white, and grey. It looked rather attractive in this combination of colours and would be left in this condition until wear and tear demanded a full repaint. While at Penycae the vehicle suffered its share of Wulfrunian problems with its disc brakes and air suspension, but its idiosyncrasies were more than compensated for by its obvious modernity compared to anything used by the other 'Rhos corridor' independents (even Williams' Regal IV) or even by Crosville. The 'Wulf' made a statement about Wrights being small but innovative and gave them publicity far beyond their native territory.

The next vehicle to arrive was a new 45-seat Bedford VAM/Duple coach delivered in April 1967. While much more humdrum than the Wulfrunian, it was interesting in the sense that it replaced the 29-seat OB/Duple coach from 1948. There were still only four vehicles in the Wright fleet, but their total seating capacity had gone from 152 at the end of 1962 to 200 by the end of 1967.

The reign of the Wulfrunian lasted for more than five years but, despite the best efforts of Wrights' chief engineer Edmund Newton (the nephew of Charles Wright and the cousin of Charles' sons Michael and John – the latter had joined the family firm in the late 1960s) all good things had to come to an end. In January 1970 the 'Wulf' was replaced by a brand-new Seddon Pennine Mk IV with 48-seat bus bodywork by Seddon's Pennine Coachcraft subsidiary. As many readers will be aware the Seddon Pennine range had its own quirks, including an unfortunate tendency to head for the nearside pavement when brakes were applied too sharply. Some drivers must have wished for a return of the double-decker where the problems were for maintenance fitters rather than for drivers anxious not to kill intending passengers.

The Wulfrunian was sold to Berresford of Cheddleton in Staffordshire at a knock-down price, but was retired from active duty within days of its arrival. According to one source (a former Berresford driver), the vehicle's 'heavy' steering frightened the life out of the normally fearless Jim Berresford during a test-drive occasioned by complaints from his staff. He returned to the depot, parked it at the rear of the premises, and it remained there until after his death in 1987 – possibly as a reminder of the 'beware Greeks bearing gifts' philosophy widely shared by bus company proprietors.

It was subsequently rescued from Cheddleton by a group of preservationists connected to the Greater Manchester Transport Society, their intention being to restore it to Bury Corporation livery. Sadly, its apparent salvation would lead to its downfall. While parked at Manchester's Hyde Road depot, still in Wright's two-tone blue livery and awaiting remedial work, it was rammed by a driver training bus and its bodywork declared a write-off. The chassis alone survives. It was a tragic end for such an historic and widely loved vehicle.

Between 1975 and 1981 Wrights' coaching fleet gradually expanded from three vehicles to five as the two Commer Avenger IVs were replaced by four new Volvos. A fifth new Volvo, a B58 bus with 51-seat Plaxton Bustler bodywork, arrived in March 1982 and replaced the kerb-diving Seddon Pennine. Few mourned the departure of the latter as they had the demise of its double-deck predecessor.

After the death of Charles Wright in 1979 his son Michael had decided to leave the bus company and to establish his own garage in Penycae. Michael's brother John had become the new proprietor, and under his leadership the company had changed its fleet-name from Wrights Coaches to 'Wrights of Wrexham' (the registered address had moved from the depot in Penycae to a solicitors' office in Wrexham town centre) and then to 'The Wright Company' – the latter change accompanied by the introduction of a dramatic new livery of dark blue and white with red relief.

With deregulation fast approaching John Wright bought the company's second ever double-decker, a Park Royal-bodied Fleetline acquired from West Midlands PTE in November 1984. Another double-decker turned up at Penycae in July 1985 and the contrast between the second-hand Fleetline and the newcomer could hardly have been any greater. B183 FDM was a brand-new Volvo B10MD with 78-seat dual-purpose bodywork by East Lancs. and represented an enormous investment for such a small operator. If the intention was to make Crosville's local fleet look old-fashioned again then the mission was a success.

In 1938 Wright of Penycae made the bold decision to buy a brand-new service bus in the shape of Grose-bodied Dodge SBF BCA 367. It was the first vehicle to carry the operator's well-known two tone blue livery and had more than paid for itself by the time it was replaced by an OB bus in 1949. After leaving Wright it passed to Noble of nearby Rhosllanerchrugog and then, in 1952, to Ashley of Dawley in Shropshire. Withdrawn by them in 1955 it found further use as a mobile shop. *(DJ Stanier)*

And here is the OB/Mulliner bus which replaced the Dodge, FUN 939, seen in Wrexham awaiting departure to Penycae. The OB gave 14 years of service to Wright and this photograph was taken on 4th May 1963, one month before its replacement by the Commer-Beadle shown in the next but one illustration. *(DJ Stanier)*

In 1959 HV Burlingham decided that their coach body for 'lightweight' front-engined chassis needed a facelift. Unfortunately, it seems that the cosmetic surgeon involved was visually handicapped. The result was this bizarre design, known to the coachbuilder's employees as 'The Pig'. It was rapidly deleted from the catalogue at the end of the year. Most were built on Bedford or Ford chassis, but Wright took one on a Commer Avenger IV, TCA 988, seen here at the Penycae depot. If possible the higher floor level of the Avenger (and the added front end chromework) made it even uglier. *(Joe Burns Collection)*

The unfortunate appearance of 'The Pig' did not discourage Wright from trying another Commer product as the proprietor liked the fuel economy of the TS3 two-stroke engine. In June 1963 this Commer-Beadle T48 Rochester coach, 26 LHX, arrived from Avis Coaches in London N6. It replaced the OB bus but its stay at Penycae was short-lived. In August 1964 it was sent to Howell & Withers in exchange for Wulfrunian double-decker LEN 101. *(Peter Yeomans)*

At the time of deregulation in October 1986 the Wright fleet included five coaches, one single-deck bus, and the two double-deckers – eight vehicles in total. Things were about to change. In November a Park Royal-bodied Leyland 'TN' Titan double-decker arrived from Greater Manchester Transport, and six more would come from the same source during 1987 along with an MCW-bodied Bristol VRT3 from West Midlands. This sudden influx of vehicles was made necessary by Wright's introduction of route X1 from Wrexham to Llangollen, in direct competition with Crosville.

Three second-hand Leyland National single-deckers were bought during 1988 (two from Cynon Valley and one from Halton) and put to work on the Penycae service, allowing the double-deckers to be concentrated on the X1. Two second-hand Leyland Leopard/Alexander Y type buses came from the Scottish Bus Group in 1989, but the big surprise of that year was the purchase of two brand-new 51-seat Leyland Lynx buses. They replaced the solitary VRT and the first of the Greater Manchester Titans. A third new Lynx single-decker was delivered in 1990, followed in 1991 by a fourth second-hand Leyland National, this time from South Yorkshire.

By then the Wright fleet had swollen to more than 20 vehicles and in October 1991 the company introduced the X2 between Wrexham and Oswestry, once again competing with a trunk service of the major operator in the region. A full-scale 'bus war' soon developed with fares being slashed and frequencies increased on both sides. To make matters worse from Wrights' viewpoint, some other local independents joined the fray, with both Bryn Melyn (qv) and Vale of Llangollen Travel becoming active on the crucial sector between Wrexham and Llangollen. In 1992 Wrights made a substantial loss, and the pattern was repeated in the first three quarters of 1993.

In November 1993 John Wright decided to cease trading at the end of that year, and to retire to a new home in the south of England. His decision was unwelcome but completely understandable, and the withdrawal of Wrights' services helped others (notably Bryn Melyn) to survive as capacity fell back to an economically viable level. For most of us of a certain age the abiding memory of Wrights is not of the brash deregulation era Titans and Lynxes, but of a gentler age when a tiny independent bought a large Wulfrunian and managed to make it go almost as reliably as a normal bus. A recent suggestion on a website that LEN 101's chassis should have a replica of its original bodywork built has my vote, but is there anybody out there brave enough (and rich enough) to attempt such a recreation? It seems highly doubtful, but it would be magnificent.

PART THREE

BUSINESS & PLEASURE

Mention has already been made of the immaculately painted double-deckers operated by P&O Lloyd of Bagillt on works services in Flintshire, but elsewhere in North Wales there were fewer such operators – dedicated exclusively to "restricted" services – than in most parts of Great Britain. Even the Lloyd fleet was comparatively small and rarely exceeded a dozen double-deckers at any given time. By 1971 the Foden and the Crossley illustrated on the opposite page had gone, and Lloyd's "works bus" fleet consisted of three Massey-bodied double-deckers bought new in 1955-9 (two Guy Arab IVs and a Leyland PD3), five second-hand PD2s (from Trent, Southdown, and Maidstone & District), and an AEC Regent V acquired from Devon General, a total of nine vehicles. Second-hand PD3s, Atlanteans, and Fleetlines would provide the next generation of the operator's rolling stock.

The Lloyd fleet was still a large one in comparison to its independent rivals for the Flintshire works traffic, with second-place Hollis of Queensferry in possession of four double-deckers in 1971 (all ex-Southport Corporation PD2s), and third-place Phillips of Bagillt only three. The local steelworks and textile factories were already in decline by the early 1970s (at least in terms of employee numbers and the percentage of those using public transport), but changes in the Welsh educational system brought additional schools journeys by way of compensation and Lloyd's double-deck fleet continued to thrive.

Further west in Caernarvonshire most works journeys were covered by special timings on existing stage carriage services, so the quarries at Dinorwic were catered for by Deiniolen Motors, and those in the Bethesda area by Purple. Across the Menai Strait in Anglesey there were many double-deckers employed over the years to carry workers to major construction projects (such as the Wylfa nuclear power station) but most of these were owned by the contractors involved rather than local companies. In 1971 there were only seven double-deckers actually registered to owners on the island, and these were divided between five different operators.

Elsewhere in the region only south-eastern Denbighshire had a significant cluster of 'works bus' operators. The coalmines and other industrial sites in the Wrexham and Dee Valley areas provided work for such companies as Williams & Davies of Southsea (with four double-deckers in 1971 including two ex-Crosville Lodekkas) and Vale of Llangollen Tours of Cefn Mawr (with four all-Leyland PD2s). VLT would soon move on to AEC Renowns (from Barton and Greater Manchester PTE - the latter ex-North Western) and would also operate the unique 36ft Fleetline double-decker built for Walsall Corporation.

Famous Names In Coaching

Crosville competed for excursion and private-hire work in all of the coastal resorts and in most of the inland market towns, leaving a much smaller piece of cake to be divided amongst local businesses. Bangor, Caernarvon, and Pwllheli had no large operators dedicated entirely to coaching activity as a result although local stage carriage operators such as Purple, Whiteway, and Caelloi respectively held a share of the market. Further east in Llandudno the higher footfall of tourists resulted in the prosperity of two well-known local coach operators, Royal Red and "The Creams". The latter was associated with Yelloway of Rochdale.

The Colwyn Bay area included the surviving remnant of the Pye group. John Pye had started his firm as a local bus company based at Heswall in Cheshire, but after the sale of his stage carriage routes to Crosville concentrated on the coaching operations in coastal Denbighshire. The company later acquired Hancock of Old Colwyn and both companies became associated with Caelloi of Pwllheli in the 1960s before being "bought back" by the Pye family and their associates in 1971.

Moving back into Flintshire, Rhyl United Coachways attracted a large number of bus enthusiast admirers for its well-kept fleet of elderly petrol-engined Bedfords. These machines offered a pleasant contrast to the Bristol SC4LK "coaches" which Crosville used on many excursions. A bad bus became a horrible coach.

In south-eastern Denbighshire most of the local independents with stage carriage routes were also active in coaching, leaving little room for niche coach operators. One notable exception was provided by Hanmer of Southsea, later acquired by GHA Coaches along with Vale of Llangollen and Bryn Melyn. GHA and its various subsidiaries have filled the coaching void left in the area by Crosville's absorption into Arriva.

P & O Lloyd operated many double-deckers of AEC, Daimler, Guy, and Leyland manufacture over the years, but these two vehicles were to remain unique. On the left is Foden PVD6/Massey FDM 568, bought new in 1949, and to the right is the rear end of Crossley DD42/Willowbrook LVO 782. The Crossley had started life with Baker Bros of Warsop, passing to East Midland in 1953 as fleet number D95, and then to Lloyd in September 1960. *(Author's Collection)*

Roberts Coaches of Cefn Mawr was established in the 1920s. In addition to its coaching interests the company operated works services to three local collieries. The three sons of Theophilus Roberts established their own separate business in 1965 by buying the coaching interests of Bryn Melyn and renaming their acquisition as Vale of Llangollen Tours. The three PD2s acquired from Great Yarmouth (one owned by Roberts Coaches, two by VLT) carried both companies' titles. Here are all three (EX 6563/6570/7550) at the Cefn Mawr depot. *(Author's Collection)*

Eric Morris of Arvonia Garage in Llanrug (near Caernarvon) operated two works services to the quarries at Llanberis using a variety of ageing coaches. In the mid-1960s the fleet included these Leyland PS2 Tigers. The Burlingham Sunsaloon example on the left, AJC 270, was a Caernarvonshire native while the Gurney Nutting-bodied half-cab to the right, KAD 325, had been acquired from Cottrell of Mitcheldean in March 1962. *(Geoff Lumb)*

Royal Red of Llandudno liked Commer Avengers, sticking with the marque from 1951 until the delivery of its final Mark IV example in 1962. This is HUN 563, a Mark I with Churchill bodywork acquired from its first owner, Roberts of Abergele, and seen at the Red Garage premises in Llandudno. After its decade of Commers Royal Red would turn to Duple-bodied Bedford VAL14s. *(DJ Stanier)*

Pye of Colwyn Bay was probably best known for the two Metalcraft-bodied Fodens it received in 1950 (one of these is illustrated in Caelloi livery in Part One). A later delivery in the same year was this AEC Regal III with fully-fronted Harrington bodywork, GUN 132. The Fodens stayed with Pye until well into the 1960s but the Regal III was sold to The Creams of Llandudno in October 1952. *(DJ Stanier)*

Bedford SB/Duple Vega WMY 886 was new to Charing Cross Motors in 1951 and gave the London operator five years of service before migrating northwards to Rhyl United Coachways in November 1956. It was still in daily use in 1971 and has survived to the present day in preservation. *(DJ Stanier)*

PART FOUR

NORTH WALES IN COLOUR

Crosville's vehicles in the early 1920s were presented in a 'colour scheme' of unrelieved grey which might lead any armchair psychiatrist to draw their own conclusions about the company's proprietors. Coaches were later painted in dark green and grey, giving a much pleasanter effect. After the LM&SR take-over in May 1929 Crosville's livery changed to maroon with cream relief, basically the colours of its new owners, and this scheme continued until 1942 when 'The Combine' disintegrated and Crosville came under the control of the Tilling group. A new livery of 'Tilling Green' with cream relief then prevailed, and this colour scheme (reversed for coaches) survived the group's sale into state ownership in 1948. A small change came in the late 1950s when coaches (and double-deckers employed on the coastal express and open-top services) were repainted into a new livery of cream with black relief.

The lack of any normal sized municipal fleets in North Wales and the sheer preponderance of Crosville vehicles would have resulted in an almost Soviet-style uniformity without the presence of the independent operators. I can remember sitting on a bench in Rhyl (where there was neither a municipal nor independent presence) in the early 1960s, and feeling more depressed by this public transport mono-culture than a child of my age should ever have felt. At least in Llandudno there were Fodens and Guy Otters in a maroon and cream livery to relieve the boredom. Elsewhere in North Wales the picture was considerably brighter.

Pwllheli could offer vehicles from Caelloi Motors (red and cream in the early 1960s, followed by shocking pink and pale cream in the latter half of the decade and then black and cream in the 1970s), Clynnog & Trevor (bright red and pale cream), and Williams of Llithfaen (chocolate brown and cream on their PS1 Tiger, followed by maroon and cream on the 30-seat Bedford). It was all in pleasing contrast to the Tilling Green of Crosville.

Caernarvon was even better in the 1960s, offering a virtual rainbow of colour schemes. Clynnog & Trevor had their bright red and cream, Express Motors used a variety of reds and cream (depending on the source of the vehicles) for buses, and a rather startling green and pink livery for its coaches. Silver Star's original livery was blue and cream, but they too later adopted different liveries for buses and coaches with the former painted in two-tone blue and cream and the latter in mustard yellow and cream. Whiteway's fleet was delightfully old-fashioned and varied, but their over-literal interpretation of the company's name (white overall with no relief) did little to enhance the appearance of their vehicles. Somehow, amid all the other colours it didn't matter.

Bangor was a dark red town from an independent perspective with the jointly managed Deiniolen and Purple fleets both favouring the colour, as did the Penmaenmawr Motor Co further to the east until changing its livery to a rather fetching dark blue and grey in the second half of the 1960s. The Llandudno & Colwyn Bay Electric Railway also chose a red livery (although the precise shade varied from one vehicle to the next), as did Phillips of Holywell whose vehicles always seemed rather dull by comparison to those of the neighbouring works bus fleet of P&O Lloyd in their gleaming pale cream with red trim.

In Wrexham and the rest of southern Denbighshire blue fleets were in the majority, with differing shades of the colour being used by Bryn Melyn, Chaloner, Evans, Johnson, Peters, Williams, and Wright. Phillips of Rhostyllen was the principal dissenter, using a combination of red and cream very similar to that of its (unrelated) namesake in Holywell. Another dissenter from the consensus was Meredith & Jesson which went from primrose and cream to an unrelieved cream similar to that employed by Wallace Arnold during the early 1960s. Although not quite as colourful as Castle Square in Caernarvon, King Street bus station in Wrexham came a close second.

DCN 861, a 1954 Tiger Cub with 44-seat Weymann Hermes bus bodywork, came to Caelloi Motors from Northern General in April 1968. As can be seen, its front end was immediately customised by the addition of a rectangular radiator grille and reports vary concerning the functionality of this modification. It is seen here at Caelloi's West End Garage in Pwllheli with VAL14/Duple Vega Major coach SRN 919 visible to its right. *(Ross Pattison)*

Two months later a second Tiger Cub bus arrived from the Northern General fleet, but on this occasion with Saunders-Roe bodywork. DCN 853 is also at the West End Garage with SRN 919 to its left and Reliance/Plaxton 41-seater NCB 915 to its right. The Reliance was one of three identical coaches acquired from Ribblesdale of Blackburn in 1969 – the other two joined the Caelloi subsidiaries in Colwyn Bay. *(Ross Pattison)*

AEC Reliance bus 255 BKM was one of four 42-seaters which Clynnog & Trevor acquired from Maidstone & District between 1969 and 1971. The first to arrive had Weymann bodywork, the next two Beadle bodywork, and this one a Harrington unit. The other three had gone by the end of 1980 but this machine soldiered on into the new decade. *(Author's Collection)*

The first three M&D Reliances were replaced by a trio of 36ft long saloons from NBC subsidiaries. Two Reliances with 49-seat Willowbrook dual-purpose bodies, 276/7 UVO, were acquired from East Midland in 1977 and the first of that pair is shown here on its way to Pwllheli. The third M&D vehicle was replaced by a 53-seat Leyland Leopard/ Weymann bus acquired from Ribble in 1980. *(Ross Pattison)*

AEC Regal III RKU 220 was new to an unidentified Bradford operator in 1948 as a half-cab coach. By 1958 it was owned by Rhind of Wakefield and they decided to rebody the vehicle as a fully-fronted 39-seat bus to Plaxton's new Highway design. In January 1964 the Regal was sold to Deiniolen Motors and is seen here in Bangor on a short working of their Dinorwic service. *(Vic Nutton)*

Here we see Express Motors' two forward entrance Bristol 'L types' side by side in Caernarvon. FFM 524 was a 35-seat L6A half-cab, modified by its original owner Crosville before passing to Express in February 1967. The modifications to FMO 23, a 39-seat LL5G had been made by Thames Valley and included a full-front as well as the repositioned entrance. *(JT Williams Collection)*

The Penmaenmawr Motor Co used the fleet name 'Crimson Rambler' for many years and the original livery which justified this name is shown here on fully-fronted Bedford OB/Plaxton coach JC 8887. The PMC acquired the vehicle from Ellis Blue in April 1949. *(Roy Marshall)*

We saw a black and white photograph of the PMC Nimbus, 548 NLG, in Part One. Here it is again in the later blue and silvery grey livery, but the really interesting thing is discovered by counting the side windows! The vehicle is seen close to Manchester's Central Station while operating the weekly 'shoppers' express' service from Penmaenmawr. *(Tony Beasley)*

This 1961 Tiger Cub with Willowbrook dual-purpose bodywork, VCH 170, came to Purple Motors from Trent in 972. The sister fleet of Deiniolen received an identical vehicle. Having previously displayed its telephone number '207') in route number displays, Purple decided to introduce real route numbers in the 1970s and the two services om Bethesda to Bangor became the 206 and 207. *(DJ Stanier)*

iger Cub 389 JTD, fitted with a 43-seat bus body by East Lancs, had been new to Lancaster Corporation in 1959 ut came to Purple in 1977 from Chester, its second owner. No repaint was necessary but the red Purple fleet ame behind the driver's seat, sloping with the beading, is notable, as are the bilingual titles in blue amidships. *Martyn Hearson)*

Bedford YMT/Duple Dominant bus BEY 7W was new to Purple in 1981. The 53-seater is seen outside the operator's Castle Garage base in Bethesda with ex-London DMS Fleetline MLK 670L visible to the right. The DMS arrived in 1980 and was Purple's first double-decker since the sale of the Arab III in 1966. *(Martyn Hearson)*

And here is an everyday vehicle in the midst of spectacular scenery. NCC 885L, a 53-seat Bedford YRT/Plaxton Elite coach, was new to Purple Motors in 1973. By then, additional blue trim had been added to the ruby red and pale cream livery. *(DJ Stanier)*

ristol SC4LK NBL 732, new in 1957 to Thames Valley as their fleet number 775, was acquired by Express Motors February 1970. As the vehicle was already in an approximation of Express's red and cream livery no repaint as considered necessary, but eight months after its arrival Express sold its stage services (and three vehicles, cluding this one) to Silver Star. Seen here in Caernarvon, shortly after the change of ownership and still in hames Valley colours, the vehicle was soon repainted into the blue livery. *(JT Williams Collection)*

ilver Star's first two SC4LKs had started life with Eastern National (the second came via KW of Daventry in 1967), nd the third (above) had arrived from Thames Valley via Express Motors. The company's fourth and last SC4LK as another Eastern National machine but came to Silver Star from its second owner, Cumberland Motor Services, 1971. 606 JPU is seen in Caernarvon in company with Whiteway's SB13/Duple Bella Vega coach ELU 509C. *JT Williams Collection)*

Four of Silver Star's Bristols (three SC4LKs and an RELH6G coach) had been new to Eastern National but th one, MW6G/ECW coach EDV 510D, came from Western National in 1979. As this view in Caernarvon show the mustard and cream coach livery suited the vehicle better than its previous colour schemes while under stat ownership. It was sold for preservation in April 1985. *(JT Williams Collection)*

Awaiting departure in Caernarvon are two Silver Star AECs. Reliance/Weymann dual-purpose vehicle 334 NK new in 1961 to Maidstone & District, later served with Booth & Fisher and the South Yorkshire PTE before comin to Silver Star in 1980 as part of a seven vehicle 'job lot'. Pennine-bodied Swift TDK 547K, new to SELNEC in 197 arrived from Greater Manchester Transport in August 1981. *(Martyn Hearson)*

We glimpsed ELU 509C in an earlier picture. A Leyland-engined Bedford SB13 with a 41-seat Duple Bella Vega coach body, it had been new to Grey-Green of London in 1965 and featured that operator's favoured 'roof box' destination display. In July 1970 it was sold to Williams Transport Services Ltd, the Caernarvon based affiliate of Whiteway, and is seen here at the depot in Waenfawr operating a 'Sherpa' leisure route with 'on hire to Whiteway' in its nearside display. *(JT Williams Collection)*

This rural idyll is Williams' depot in Llithfaen and the vehicles are Bedford C5Z1/Duple (Midland) bus OTY 208 and B3/Duple Super Vega coach HCC 850. The two white smudges visible at the left of the photograph are sheep. *(Geoff Lumb via Lawrence Corrieri)*

We saw this Bristol K5G (AJA 160) in black and white in Part Two, parked in Glyn Ceiriog and still wearing basi[c] North Western livery. Here it is in Glyn Ceiriog again but with the red areas of its livery expanded to take in the roc[f] and upper deck window surrounds. As far as is known the machine never received Bryn Melyn's blue and crea[m] livery despite a five year stay in the fleet. *(Geoff Lumb)*

By April 1976, when this SB5 bus was delivered new to Chaloner of Moss, the Duple (Midland) name had bee[n] abandoned and the products of the Leicestershire factory were all being marketed under the Willowbrook bran[d.] As PCA 331P illustrates, only the name had changed. Later in its life it acquired a pale blue roof, resulting in a live[ry] very similar to that of Silver Star. *(Author's Collection)*

nd here is photographic evidence that Meredith & Jesson used their magnificent AEC Regal IV/Bellhouse Hartwell andmaster coach, HCA 650, on their stage service from Cefn Mawr to Wrexham. There were two versions of the andmaster body, and personally I prefer the variation with breast shaped headlight fairings, but we'll say no more bout that. HCA 650 was nice too! *(Roy Marshall)*

eters of Llanarmon-yn-Lal sold their Crossley observation coach in February 1962, but its replacement was lmost equally rare. MXB 38, seen at the depot, was a Tilling-Stevens Express Mk II with a Meadows engine and coach body of Duple's 'Vega lookalike' design. It came to Peters from Banfield of London SE7. *(Vic Nutton)*

In October 1965 Phillips of Holywell replaced its ex-Wallasey PD1 with an ex-Wallasey PD2, CHF 565. The Burlingham body on this vehicle had originally been fitted to a pre-war TD4c chassis in 1949 (one of six thus rebodied). After the TD4c chassis reached the ends of their lives in 1956, the 1949 bodies were transferred to s brand-new PD2/10 chassis. Also seen in this depot shot is Seddon Mk 17 bus TDM 855. *(JT Williams Collection)*

Ten years after the arrival of the Mk 17 Phillips bought another Seddon, albeit less rare and less attractive to driver and enthusiast alike. XDM 872H was a Seddon Pennine Mk IV with Pennine Coachcraft bus bodywork very similar to that on the 100 rear-engined versions then being supplied to Crosville. It was new to Phillips in August 1969 and is seen at the Holywell depot. *(JT Williams Collection)*

Phillips of Rhostyllen bought this 1947 vintage PS1 Tiger bus with 35-seat rear entrance BBW bodywork, to the CW design, from Red & White in August 1959. EU 8390 was withdrawn from use in March 1964. An identical PS1 Tiger went from Red & White to Bryn Melyn along with an Albion Valkyrie/BBW bus shown in Part Two. *(JT Williams Collection)*

Later deliveries to the Phillips fleet were of a more mundane nature. SUN 594J was a Ford R192 with a 45-seat bus body redesignated as the Willowbrook 001, although indistinguishable from the preceding Duple (Midland) design. It came to Rhostyllen when new in October 1970 and is seen in Wrexham bus station en route to 'Rhos', the local abbreviation for Rhosllanerchrugog. *(JT Williams Collection)*

Ford R192/Plaxton Derwent bus LAW 987P was new to Price (Excelsior) of Wrockwardine Wood in Shropshire 1975. In August 1981 it was sold to Williams of Ponciau and is seen here in need of a wash in Wrexham bus statio bound for 'Rhos'. *(JT Williams Collection)*

The East Yorkshire registration of this 55-seat Bedford YMT bus (UKH 170W) reveals that it originally served i bodybuilder, Plaxton of Scarborough, as a demonstrator. Equipped with Plaxton's new Bustler body design, it wa acquired by Williams of Ponciau in December 1981. *(JT Williams Collection)*

hots of Wright's Wulfrunian LEN 101 'in service' after repaint into the fleet's two-tone blue livery proved surprisingly
ird to find, although there were plenty of it rotting in Berresford's yard after sale to the Cheddleton operator. In this
ss than perfect image it is seen leaving Wrexham for Penycae. *(Berwyn Prys Jones Collection)*

seems that the Wright family loved a challenge as they replaced the Wulfrunian (a type which made most
)erators run away in fright) with this later 'Blunderbus', a Seddon Pennine Mk IV with a Pennine Coachcraft body.
JN 273H was new to them in January 1970. The hand-written sign in the windscreen reads 'Please pay as you
iter' – the Wulf had carried a conductor. *(Author's Collection)*

In the 1960s the contract works service fleet of P & O Lloyd included four Massey-bodied double-deckers boug[ht] new (a Foden PVD6, two Guy Arab IVs, and a Leyland PD3) as well as various second-hand specimens. By th[e] mid-1980s all of the double-deckers were second-hand but included such gems as Alexander-bodied PD3/2 EW[S] 833D (ex Edinburgh) and East Lancs-bodied PD2A/27 FHG 162E (ex Burnley, Colne, and Nelson JTC). The scen[e] is the depot at Bagillt. *(Martyn Hearson)*

I mentioned in the Introduction that my father's mother was a Jones from Flint. Here is another one to close th[e] book! Bedford VAL14/Strachan 52-seater AJA 139B was one of ten delivered to North Western in 1964. In th[is] shot it is flanked by two Phillips of Holywell Bedfords, VAM14/Duple (Midland) bus NDM 950E to the right and SB[?] Duple (Northern) Firefly coach 103 FDM to the left. *(Martyn Hearson)*